THE BALLAD OF
PLÁCIDA ROMERO

En el dia de San Lore[nzo]
Serea de las seis del d[ia]
asi seria yo pienso
cuando esto nos suse[dio]
que vi a mi Esposo
como pues lo resistir[ia]
A Dios lla.
Hay Esposo desgracia[do]
a Dios y no compa[ñero]
y_ui sa no tenias cuña[dos]
ni parientes en Cuber[o]
puesto quedastes tira[do]
adentro de un galli[nero]
A Dios lla.
Este mundo escandalo[so]

THE BALLAD OF PLÁCIDA ROMERO

A Woman's Captivity & Redemption

AULTON E. "BOB" ROLAND

Foreword by
JERRY D. THOMPSON

Introduction by
ENRIQUE R. LAMADRID

Afterword by
LESLIE MARMON SILKO

MUSEUM OF NEW MEXCO PRESS
SANTA FE

© 2022 Aulton E. "Bob" Roland. Foreword, introduction, afterword © each respective author. *All rights reserved*. No part of this book may be reproduced in any form or by any means whatsoever without the express written consent of the publisher.

Director: Anna Gallegos
Editorial director: Lisa Pacheco
Art director and project manager: David Skolkin
Designed by: David Skolkin

Composition: Set in New Caledonia and Albertus
Manufactured in Korea
10 9 8 7 6 5 4 3 2 1

Library of Congress Control Number: 2022936406
ISBN 978-0-89013-672-0

Museum of New Mexico Press
PO Box 2087
Santa Fe, New Mexico 87504
mnmpress.org

Frontispiece: Rosa Trujillo in 1986 holding a photograph of Plácida (*right*) and her daughter, Manuelita (*left*). Photograph by Miguel Gandert.

CONTENTS

FOREWORD *by Jerry D. Thompson* 7
INTRODUCTION *by Enrique R. Lamadrid* 11
CORRIDO DE PLÁCIDA ROMERO 15

1 Background 25
2 The Tragic Capture of Plácida Romero 37
3 The Flight to Mexico 43
4 In Mexico and Return Home 47
5 The Military Pursuit 55
6 The Aftermath 61
7 Variations of the Plácida Story 69

AFTERWORD
A Laguna Connection *by Leslie Marmon Silko* 73

ACKNOWLEDGMENTS 81

APPENDIXES

1 Original Spanish Corrido Transcription as presented to Arthur Bibo 87
2 Arthur G. Bibo Eulogy *by John L. Kessell* 97
3 Descendants of María Plácida Romero 99
4 Newspaper Articles on Plácida's Escape 101
5 Act of the Legislative Assembly of the Territory of New Mexico, 1882 104
6 Newspaper Articles Pertaining to Navajo Agent Galen Eastman 106
7 *Albuquerque Daily Journal* Articles 110
8 Las Cosas Perdidas de Rancho Armijo *by Carol A. Macaulay-Jameson* 113

NOTES AND HISTORICAL COMMENTARY 121
BIBLIOGRAPHY 133
INDEX 137

FOREWORD

Jerry D. Thompson

Early on the morning of August 8, 1881, seven Apache warriors and twelve Navajo raiders made their way on horseback down a piñon-and-ponderosa–shrouded plateau in west central New Mexico Territory to the rock and terrones La Cebolla Ranch house of Domingo and Plácida Romero Gallegos. The raiders were led by sixty-six-year-old Nana (Kas-tziden) who was determined to avenge the death of his nephew Victorio, the legendary Mimbreño Apache leader, who had been killed ten months earlier along with most of his warriors at Cerro Tres Castillos in the Chihuahuan desert, seventy miles south of El Paso, by Mexican troops under the command of colonel Joaquín Terrazas. Several of the surviving Apaches had been executed and over ninety Apache women and children enslaved. Only Nana and a handful of Mimbreños managed to escape the desert carnage. In early July 1881, Nana and fifteen warriors had splashed across the Río Grande near Fort Quitman, Texas, and headed north into New Mexico. The two-month foray of vengeance that followed, ranging over more than a thousand miles in some of the most inhospitable terrain in the Southwest, became legendary as "Nana's Raid."

At La Cebolla Ranch the raiders killed Domingo Gallegos along with a ranch hand, José María Vargas, carried off Plácida Romero, and rode off into the timbered high country to the east. Near Blue Water Vega, not far from La Cebolla Ranch, Plácida was forced to hand over her nine-month-old daughter to a group of Navajos. Eventually carried into the deserts of Chihuahua, Plácida made an amazing escape in September 1881, and returned to New Mexico, where she was reunited with her family at the small rock-and-adobe outpost of Cubero. Here the story of her capture, heartbreaking agony, and miraculous escape was passed from generation to generation and became the subject of one of the most fascinating and captivating traditional native ballads in New Mexico history.

New Mexico Territory in the nineteenth century was a land unlike any other. Here a colonial tradition of capture and servitude stretched across cultures and meshed to form a slave system in which victims performed labor for their masters. Slave and livestock raiding became a way of life among the Apache, Comanche, Kiowa, Navajo, Ute, and Spanish alike. In the mid nineteenth century civilizations collided in the heart of the borderlands, Native Americans were subjugated, cultures blended, and violence swept over the land. Culturally and geographically isolated and with divided loyalties, the people of New Mexico, often poor, came to develop a mistrust of outside authority.

Caught in the clash of empires were the Native Americans. In the violence that was an integral part of the history of the Southwest, wealthy traders, farmers, and stockmen came to hold thousands of Native Americans as slaves. Raiders traveling west from the Río Grande carried off hundreds of Navajo slaves, especially women and children. So lucrative was the trade that the territorial legislature legalized Indian slavery. By the time of the Civil War, almost every wealthy family in the territory, including the governor and most territorial officials, held at least one Navajo slave. Comanches sweeping across the western fringes of the Llano Estacado also carried away captives, as did the Apaches who emerged out of the high desert and rugged mountains west of the Río Grande.

For centuries the Native Americans of New Mexico made war on the Spanish and then the Mexicans and finally on the Americans. In several instances, the United States Army made feeble attempts to prevent abductions but devoted more effort to keeping the Navajos from raiding the Hispanic villages in the Río Grande watershed. Enslaved Navajo and other indigenous people were frequently baptized into the Catholic Church and assimilated into Hispanic culture, given the name of the owner's family, sometimes even intermarrying with *nuevomexicanos*, and in rare instances, were legally adopted and allowed to inherit property.

Slave raiding reached new heights during the Civil War, and the isolated village of Seboyeta, not far from Cubero, became a place of great agony for the Navajo. Here they were held before being taken to the Río Grande and sold for as little as $100. In 1860, the territory's Kentucky-born governor, Henry Connelly, who one critic said knew as much about the "Constitution as a horse does about Latin," held four slaves and two peons. Prior to the war he had also owned African American slaves.

Even before the agonizing Long Walk and the humiliating captivity at the Bosque Redondo, Navajo captives continued to be seized. By the end of the Civil War between five and six thousand Navajos were held as slaves in New Mexico. In 1868, Navajo chief Barboncito told general William Tecumseh Sherman that at least half his tribe was held as slaves. That same year, 363 peons or slaves were freed in Taos, Santa Fe, and Río Arriba Counties alone. In 1872, Chief Manuelito complained to general Oliver O. Howard that hundreds of Navajo children were still in captivity.

Even after the passage of the Thirteenth Amendment to the US Constitution in 1865 that ended slavery and involuntary servitude, peonage, a "curse upon the country" as one observer put it, was so widespread in New Mexico that the US Congress passed an antipeonage law on March 2, 1867, that was aimed directly at the territory: "The holding of any person to servitude or labor under the system known as peonage is abolished and forever prohibited in the territory of New Mexico . . . and all acts, laws . . . made to establish, maintain, or enforce, directly or indirectly, the voluntary or involuntary service or labor of any persons as peons, in liquidation of any debt or obligation, or otherwise are declared null and void."

In the heart of a harsh, starkly beautiful landscape, on the eastern rim of the malpais where the high desert stretches to the horizon and the spring winds whistle through the canyonlands, Aulton E. "Bob" Roland, with energy, perseverance, and an uncanny feel for the landscape and its people, helps bring to life one of the last chapters in the Hispanic–Native American world of the late nineteenth century—the agonizing yet heartwarming story of Plácida Romero. Arriving in Albuquerque from the Midwest on his eighth birthday in 1949, Bob fell in love with the vast deserts, colorful canyons, and rugged mountains of the Southwest. A graduate of Highland High School, Bob went on to technical school at what is now the Oklahoma State University Institute of Technology and then worked as a technical illustrator for ten years. In 1971, he bought the Arty Bibo Los Pilares Ranch headquarters and forty acres of land near La Angostura, close to what is today the picturesque El Malpais National Monument on the western edge of the Acoma Indian Reservation. At the same time Roland turned his technical skills toward mining engineering and worked in the uranium mines near Grants and later at the Waste Isolation Pilot Plant near Carlsbad. Also during his mining career he spent several years at Crownpoint, New Mexico, working with the Navajo people there and soaking up their culture. In 2001, Bob retired from mining and returned to the land of vast vistas and squeaky windmills on the windswept Colorado Plateau to settle with his wife Nelcine and pursue his interests in New Mexico history.

Bob first heard the story of Plácida Romero when he met Arthur "Arty" Bibo in 1961. With his knowledge of the land and his love for the Native American and Hispanic people of the area, Bob helped Arty in researching the events behind the story. Over time and after Arty's death, Bob found the exact locations of the events of Nana's raid, some of them in very remote locations and in Mexico, even chartering airplanes in some cases to aid in his searching. He also corrected a number of historical misconceptions concerning the events of the bloody raid, discovering in the process that Plácida Romero never recovered her abducted daughter, Trinidad Gallegos, although the child had grown up with the Navajo people near Prewitt only fifty miles from Cubero, where Plácida lived, died, and is buried.

The Ballad of Plácida Romero: A Woman's Captivity & Redemptiong is terrific—a captivating, deeply moving, and incisive piece of New Mexico history. It is a provocative and uplifting slice of survival and suspense on a fragile frontier in New Mexico Territory in the late nineteenth century.

INTRODUCTION

Enrique R. Lamadrid

>What she is leaving with us-
>the stories and remembered accounts-
>is primarily what she was able to tell
>and what we are able to remember.
>
>As with any generation
>the oral tradition depends upon each person
>listening and remembering a portion
>and it is together-
>all of us remembering what we have heard together-
>that creates the whole story
>the long story of the people.
>
>I remember only a small part.
>But this is what I remember.
>
>LESLIE MARMON SILKO, *Storyteller*

THE TAKING OF CAPTIVES in the desperate Apache wars of the 1880s brought suffering and controversy to the New Mexico Territory and the states of northern Mexico. The problem was of such a magnitude that an entire article of the Treaty of Guadalupe Hidalgo, Article XI, was dedicated to the disposition of transnational captives and the responsibility of the United States to repatriate them, punish their captors, and pacify the borderlands. Early on, the American military realized what the challenges of ending these wars would be. In a November 20, 1851, letter to Brevet Major General Roger Jones, Colonel Edwin V. Sumner expressed these grave concerns: "This predatory war has been carried on for two hundred years, between the Mexicans & Indians, quite time enough to prove, that unless some change is made the war will be interminable. They steal women and children, and cattle, from each other, and in fact carry on the war, in all respects, like two Indian nations."

A dispersed population engaged in farming, ranching, and mining was vulnerable to the guerilla-style tactics of the Apaches, and the US Army was challenged and frustrated by an elusive enemy. People were incensed with the seeming inability of the military to deal with the situation, and vigilante responses often led to further tragedies. The rights and responsibilities of citizens and their government were put to question in newspapers, courts, and the territorial legislature.

The captivity of Plácida Romero in 1881 at the hands of chief Nana and a war party of Chihene Nde (Red Paint Apaches) had local, national, and international repercussions. Since it happened near the end of the Indian Wars in North America, the captivity of Plácida Romero is richly documented in multiple sources, from military records, legal documents including a deposition and a legislative memorial, to newspaper accounts and editorials, to family stories. In detail and nuance, her story is still contested, remembered, and celebrated by her descendants. Her demands for justice after her own ordeal and the murder of her husband sparked a heated controversy that swept the territory. Just what were the rights of *nuevomexicana* women under the new jurisdiction of a US Territory? At the center of the storm is the testimony of an extraordinary woman and a hauntingly beautiful ballad narrated in her voice. Captivity stories are too often propagandized and mediated. The voices of women are submerged and silenced. Not in the case of Plácida Romero.

In the Southwest borderlands, the most complex and compelling captivity stories are told about women. There were male captives taken, more boys than men, but they often assumed control of their own accounts. Since the often unspoken and unspeakable aspects of the ordeals of women captives are implied, imagined, or assumed, their voices disappear almost immediately. As a result, most captivity narratives are heavily mediated and told by interested others who feel compelled, even obsessed by the telling. The voices of captive women are quickly submerged as their testimonies are subsumed into other agendas. In the tradition of Anglo American captivity narratives, stories of survival and endurance are often laden with ideological baggage to fuel propagandistic agendas and build support for war. The Mexicano tradition of captivity stories is set in a spiritual framework of faith and redemption.

As she emerged from the deep trauma of her captivity and the frustrated attempts to recover her daughter, Plácida Romero was the first to realize how compelling her story would become to her family and community and how many would empathize with her ordeals. As we shall see, the poetics of the ballad she helped to compose proved to be the most enduring and persuasive form her story would take. The rhetorical power of the first-person narrative poem projected her voice far into the future and into oral tradition.

Over months and years, Plácida was engaged in a narrative process that has been termed "transvaluation," a process of rhetorical reframing in which her personal story of captivity and redemption acquired value and transcendent meaning to the larger community. Amy Shuman identifies two closely related impulses in this process, empathy and entitlement: "Both entitlement and empathy claims extend personal narratives beyond the personal; empathy appropriates the personal with the goal of greater understanding across experiential differences, and entitlement reclaims the personal in terms of ownership of experience."[1]

Empathy flows intuitively from the deep-seated source of emotion. But it can easily turn into nostalgia and appropriation of someone else's story. Entitlement is the reclaiming of narrative authority, based on direct experience, and links to that person who makes the testimony. Both happen with Plácida's story.

María Plácida's experiences inspired the stories of family and others who all vie for narrative and cultural authority. This is a catalog of narrative responses, with the eyewitness testimonies of La Cautiva herself and Kaywaykla, the Apache boy and grandson of Nana who witnessed the treatment of Mexican captives in Mexico at the time and places of Plácida's captivity. Successive generations of narrators embrace and shape the story as they pass it along through the families of María Plácida and her descendants—Rosa Trujillo, a granddaughter, and others—and those of her brother Cayetano. Networks of kin and community link all these people back to the establishment of the Cubero Land Grant in 1833. In New Mexico genealogy is also a "powerful cultural force" in the Hispano community with a performative element through which people locate each other and their histories in relation to place. As a component of storytelling, genealogy is a metanarrative feature that enables a narrator to construct credibility and legitimacy for the narrative.

Although genealogy is an important linkage to entitlement and narrative authority, the larger community also creates its own bonds with the story. Arthur Bibo was raised in Cubero and shared with Bob Roland a deep passion for history. Both men's close familiarity with the geography of the story are captured in topographical and verbal detail. With interests in cultural relations, music, and the mestizo legacy of New Mexico, I followed students into the story and write these words to frame what others may write and speak.

Almost immediately upon her return to Cubero, instead of retreating in shame and sorrow into the arms of her family, Plácida Romero asserted her rights in the sworn declaration that she made before Justice of the Peace Gregorio Otero. She demanded justice for the murder of her husband and named his assailants. She began a desperate and ultimately fruitless search for her infant daughter, opposed by an Indian Agent who protected her tormentors to cover his own corruption. To acquire the weight of legal testimony, her story is entirely mediated by the sympathetic local magistrate, who duly transcribes it into third-person discourse.

Three months earlier, the territorial legislature had passed an act with the basic details of the case to authorize governor Lionel Sheldon to request and finance the repatriation of Plácida and Procopio García, who were both being held by the Mexican authorities.[2] Her more detailed deposition ignited inquiries in official circles, and outrage in the court of public opinion.

In Territorial New Mexico, nuevomexicanos were beginning to assert their rights as US citizens. The Spanish-language press played a key role to "imponer a los mexicanos de nuestro Territorio al estilo americano," in getting the New Mexicans of our Territory used to the "American style" of voicing problems and opinions in the press, said the editors of the *Crónica del Río Colorado*, June 17, 1882, one of the newspapers that most closely followed the case of Plácida Romero. Published in a town near Las Vegas, New Mexico, one of the seats of political power in New Mexico, it did attract the attention of the authorities.

Governor Sheldon himself ordered Navajo Indian agent Galen Eastman to conduct an inquest. Over an entire week he interrogated Güero, one of the Navajos named in Plácida's deposition. Güero convinced Eastman that the Apaches forced him to join their war party, that he was afraid of them, and that they had killed the child, Trinidad, so she could not possibly be with Navajos as Plácida insisted. Her credibility was called into question, and she was accused of exaggerating her claims. In an impassioned commentary on this news, justice of the peace Gregorio Otero smirked that Güero was "as afraid of the Apaches as crows are of corn." Unfortunately, a desperate mother's pleas were dismissed, and he cynically adds: "Al cabo se cree más al peor Navajo que al mejor mexicano. (Finally, the worst Navajo has more credibility than the best Mexicano.)"[3]

In the end, the courageous public testimonial of a humble New Mexican woman provoked a political controversy that reached the highest circles of the Territorial government even though it failed to recover her child.

CORRIDO DE PLÁCIDA ROMERO

This ballad, as it was originally composed, contains twenty-six verses plus two different refrains and is the most complete known to date in New Mexico folklore and history. I have always marveled at the wonderful rhyming of all the stanzas in Spanish. In the original transcription, the pages do not reflect the exact verse sequence that tells the story in the correct chronological order. Apparent upon examination of the original over-a-century-old document is that the cloth-bound handmade booklet and pages have experienced considerable wear and tear. The pages obviously have been re-sewn into their cover one or more times. These repairs can partially account for how the written story has become unsequenced, since there are no page numbers in the original document. According to family sources, some years passed before the ballad was actually transcribed onto paper, having been committed to memory previously. It is also possible that Plácida was not present when the transcribing occurred. Probably the transcribers were not familiar with the true chronology of the story and thus possibly introduced errors in sequencing of verses in the original written recording process.

The order of these verses, as presented here, conforms to the way the original ballad was mostly performed and in the correct chronological sequence. Arty Bibo and I suspected this, and we later recovered a typed copy of the ballad as it was formerly sung by Felipe Trujillo, which confirmed our suspicions and thus enabled us to logically revise the presentation. A photocopy of the original Spanish unsequenced version is in appendix 1, this volume.

When Arty and I were doing our research in the 1960s, all the family members we interviewed referred to this ballad as a corrido, and we use this designation historically. However, according to Dr. Lamadrid, it is more accurate to call this ballad an *indita* in Spanish. Here I quote from his unpublished manuscript:

> The stories of Plácida Romero have been on the lips of her family and community for six generations. A few have found their way onto paper in the process of reflection and documentation called history. But these sources are ephemeral when compared to the extraordinary commemorative poetry that emerged from this story. Thanks to the power and persistence of popular poetry, deep and specific conversations on the history and culture of New Mexico are possible. The nucleus of this poetry is the female engendered voice of the *indita* ballad, a genre of narrative folk

song closely allied to the male engendered *corrido*. The highly emotive first-person voice of Plácida is heard in every single verse as she insists on telling and retelling her own story. She performed it herself as do her female descendants, so many years later.

The major difference between the Corrido and the Indita is rhetorical. Corridos are almost always set in third-person discourse, which frames first and second person exchanges as reported speech. The majority of Inditas feature first person narration in the voice of the protagonist, a simple device that lends itself to dramatic irony, especially when the character narrates her or his demise or death.

—Enrique R. Lamadrid, "La Pasión de Plácida Romero"[1]

In the following translation of the ballad the Spanish language version is reproduced as it appears in the original transcription with the spelling, capitalization, abbreviations, and punctuation remaining the same.

CORRIDO/INDITA DE PLÁCIDA ROMERO

Music Composed by – Rafael Abeyta y Romero
Words by – María Gutiérrez
Transcribed by – Melquiades Otero[2]

A Dios le pido memoria
y permiso al mundo entero
para dictar esta historia
de la Placida Romero
que tal ves sera notoria
en y fuera de Cubero.
    [Estribillo]
A Dios ya me boy
sin duda a padeser
a mis padres y a mis hijas
cuando las volveré aver.

Año de mil ochocientos
ochenta y uno llovioso
el dia de San Lorenso
quiso el todo poderoso
que me quedara sintiendo
a mi hijita y a mi esposo
    A Dios lla

Sentandonos a almorsar
se nos llego la ocacion
Quien lo avia de pensar
que esta varbara nacion
nos quisieran cautibar
y pegarnos a traicion
    A Dios lla

1. I beg God for my memory
And permission of the entire world
To tell this story
Of Plácida Romero
Who perhaps might well be famous
Inside and outside of Cubero.
    [Refrain]
Farewell I am going
Without doubt to suffer
My parents and my daughters
When will I see them again.

2. The year of 1881
A rainy San Lorenzo day
The Almighty wanted
To leave me feeling sorry
For my daughter
And my husband.
    Farewell, etc.

3. We were sitting down to breakfast
When this danger arrived
Who would have thought
That this barbarous nation
Wanted to make us captive [*]
And strike us down with treachery.
    Farewell, etc.

En el dia de San Lorenzo
serea de las seis del dia
asi seria yo pienso
cuando esto nos susedia
que vi a mi esposo muriendo
como pues lo resistia
    A Dios lla.

Hay esposo desgraciado
A Dios fino compañero
quiza no tenias cuñado
ni parientes en Cubero
pueste quedastes tirado
adentro de un gallinero
    A Dios lla.

Este mundo escandaloso
no es mas q. [que] un aparato
Sevolla Rancho famoso
porque fuistes tan ingrato
donde matan ami esposo
Y a mi q. me lleva el tato
    A Dios llá

Hay esposo de mi vida
y con que dolor murio
con una mortal heriada
que aun ni sus harmas uso
viendome salir cautiba
A Dios el alma entrego.
    A. Dios lla

4. It was the day of San Lorenzo
It must have been about 6 o'clock
Thus it was I believe
When this happened to us
That I saw my husband dying
Although he resisted it
    Farewell, etc.

5. Unfortunate husband
Farewell fond friend
Perhaps you didn't have a brother-in-law
Nor relatives in Cubero
All of a sudden you were left
    Tossed into a chicken house.
    Farewell, etc.

6. This shameful world
Is nothing more than a show
Famous Sevolla Ranch
Why were you so ungrateful?
Where they killed my husband
And el tato carried me off.[3]
    Farewell, etc.

7. Oh my beloved husband
Who died in pain
With a mortal wound
He never got to use his weapons
Although he saw me leaving captive
He gave up his soul to God.
    Farewell, etc.

Tan fuerte golpe le an dado
que con el fierro de herrar
vi sus sesos derramados
sin poderlo remediar
hey Domingo desgraciado
como no te he de llorar.
    A. D. lla

San Lorenso milagroso
por que escojistes tu dia
mostrandote reguroso
quisas lla me convenia
que mataran ami esposo
tambien a Jose M. [María]
    A. Dios llá,

A Dios Madresita fina
duelase de mi desgracia
Á Dios todos mis vesinos
Á Dios mi ogar y mi casa
Á Dios tambien a mis parientes
Á Dios Madre M.a [María] Cacia.
    A. Dios llá.

Desde el dia que salid
del paraje mas sereano
con mucho cuidado fui
cuando encumbrava alg.n llano
aver si via benir a mi
padre ho, á mi Ermano.
    A. Dios llá.

8.   They gave him such a heavy blow
    With the branding iron
    That I saw his brains scattered
    Without being able to save him
    Oh Domingo unfortunate one
    Why should I not weep for you.
        Farewell, etc.

9.   Miraculous San Lorenzo
    Why did you choose your name day
    Showing yourself to be so severe[4]
    Perhaps I deserved
    That my husband should be killed
    And also José María.
        Farewell, etc.

10. Farewell my dear mother
     Grieve over my unhappiness
     Farewell all my neighbors
     Farewell my hearth and my home
     Farewell also to my relatives
     Farewell Mother María Cacia.[5]
         Farewell, etc.

11. Since the day I departed
     From that mountain camp
     With great watchfulness I went
     When I looked down on some plain
     To see if my father or my brother
     Were to come this way.
         Farewell, etc.

En la mesa de la Escoba
sequedo mi hija querida
Hay Sierra de la Sebolla
por que fuistes tan esquiba
las piedras los palos lloran
a verme salir cautiba.
    A. Dios llá.

Llegue al Ojito Salado
con aquel dolor ardiente
como es paraje mentado
llayi [alli] esperaba la gente
Á Dios Cubero afamado
se te acabo lo valiente.
    A. Dios llá.

En las minas fue el a caso
pegue un suspiro velos
y como llegue despacio
hay bi que mataron dos
el hijo llamado Ygnacio
y su padre Juan de Dios.
    A. Dios llá,

Madre mia dolorosa
Padre mio San José
la pues madre amorosa
te lo pido por mersed
cuida a mis hijas piedosa
pues huerfanas hoy se ven.
    A Dios lla me voy

12. On the Mesa de la Escoba
    I left behind my beloved daughter
    Oh Sierra de la Sebolla
    Why were you so disdainful
    The rocks and the trees weep
    On seeing me captive.
        Farewell, etc.

13. I arrived at the Ojito Salado
    With that burning pain
    Since it is a well known camp
    People were waiting there
    Farewell famed Cubero
    Your valor has ended.[6]
        Farewell, etc.

14. In the mines there was an incident
    I gave a great sigh
    And since I arrived slowly
    There I saw that they had killed two
    A son named Ygnacio
    And his father Juan de Dios.
        Farewell, etc.

15. My sorrowful mother
    Saint Joseph
    Loving Mother
    I beg you for mercy
    Watch over my daughters with mercy
    They are becoming orphans today.
        Farewell, etc.

Madresita de la Lus
Madre de mi corason
pidele a tu hijo Jesus
me saque de esta prision
pues q. su cumbio en la crus
tenga de mi compasion.
    A. Dios llá,,

Boy sintiendo un gran dolor
porq. dejé á mis hijitas
Manuelita la mayor
cuida de tus Ermanitas
pues lla les falto el calor
quedaron huerfanitas
    A. Dios llá,,

A mi padre y a mi Ermano
les en cargo a mis hijitas
no te olvides Calletano
de tus caras sobrinitas
hay se quedan huerfanitas
en este mundo tirano.
    A. Dios llá,,

A Dios padres desgraciado
hechenme su vendicion
y esten siempre con cuidado
en cualesquiera ocacion
con estos indios malvado
esta varbara nacion
    A Dios llá,,

16. Sweet Mother of Light[7]
    Mother of my heart
    Ask your son Jesus
    To release me from this prison
    Since he died on the cross
    He will have compassion for me.
        Farewell, etc.

17. I am feeling great pain
    Because I left my daughters
    Manuelita the oldest[8]
    Care for your little sisters
    They are missing my warmth
    They were left little orphans.
        Farewell, etc.

18. To my father and my brother
    I commit my little daughters
    Don't forget Calletano
    Your beloved little nieces
    They are left little orphans there
    In this tyrannical world.[9]
        Farewell, etc.

19. Farewell unhappy parents
    Give me your blessing
    And always be careful
    In whatever undertakings
    With these accursed Indians
    This barbarous nation.
        Farewell, etc.

A Dios Madresita mia
A Dios mi querido Padre
jusgen como quedaria
con este crecido alarde
viendo ayi mi compania
revoleandose en su sangre.
    A. Dios llá,,
	20. Farewell beloved mother
	    Farewell my dear father
	    Judge how it would be
	    With this growing cry
	    Seeing there my companions
	    Writhing in their own blood.
	        Farewell, etc.

El dia q. lla llegue
Serea de San Buenabentura
A Dios le pedi mersed
como una infelis Criatura
y al patriarca San José
tambien a la Virjen Pura
    [Estribillo Nuevo]
Ho Dios lla meciento libres
por tu gran poder
Y a mis padres y a mis hijas
espero volver aver.
	21. The day that I arrived
	    It was close to San Buenaventura
	    I begged God's mercy
	    Like an unhappy creature
	    And also of the patriarch St. Joseph
	    And of the pure virgin.
	    [New Refrain]
	    Oh God I feel free
	    Because of your great power
	    I expect to see my parents
	    And my daughters again.

Veite sinco de Setiembre
Ya Dios se compadecio
Ya le pedi humildem. te
y el mis suplicas holló
ayi nos sintio la gente
y al momento nos sigio.
    O Dios llá, meciento libres
	22. The 25th of September[10]
	    God finally took pity
	    I had asked Him humbly
	    And he heard my entreaties
	    The people there heard us
	    And soon followed us.
	    Oh God, etc.

Luego que reconocid
Ser gente la que venia
que salieramos de alli
parese llegado el dia
no te retires de mi
dije ha Procopio García
    Oh. Dios llá,,
	23. Then when I recognized
	    The people who were coming
	    It seemed the day had come
	    That we could leave there
	    Don't leave me
	    I said to Procopio García.
	    Oh God, etc.

Si la corte selestial	24. If the celestial court
esclame á San Augustin	Exclaims to San Augustín
propucieron terminar	Proposing to end
de mi cautiberio al fin	My captivity finally
me propongo no olvidar	I resolve never to forget
el Cañon de San Juaquin.	San Joaquín Canyon.
Oh Dios llá.	Oh God, etc.
En que trabajos me he visto	25. In what travail I've seen myself
con estos indios tiranos	With these tyrannical Indians
ho Sierra Madre del Cristo	Oh Sierra Madre del Cristo[11]
donde Dios me dio sus manos	Where God gave me his help
y donde libre me he visto	And where I found myself free
y en las manos de Cristianos	And in the hands of Christians.
Ho. Dios llá.	Oh God, etc.
Ya yo quisas me olvide	26. I guess I've already forgotten
lla no se acuerdan de mi	Nor do they remember me
llo luego les noticie	Since I notified them
desde el dia que sali	From the day I left
lla me toca padeser	It is my lot to suffer
con este signo nasi	I was born under this sign.[12]
Ho Dios lla,	Oh God, etc.

END

Arthur G. Bibo with his favorite horse, Zuni, at his ranch in the Cebollita Valley (ca. 1950s). Photograph by John Barnes (author's collection).

1
Background

> Victorio had killed many, but the count was small in comparison to the number of lives Nana exacted in retaliation for Victorio's death. This was conceded at one time by Geronimo and also by Juh, a Nednhi chief, who terrorized southern Arizona for years.
>
> —JAMES KAYWAYKLA, *In the Days of Victorio*

THIS WORK TO SAVE AND CORRECT New Mexico history explores and evolves around the story of Plácida Romero, a nuevomexicana who was taken captive and whose husband, Domingo Gallegos, was murdered at their Cebolla Springs Ranch (also known as Rancho Cebolla) by an Apache war party led by Nana during a raid into south and central New Mexico in 1881. This incursion, one of the last major Apache raids into the territory, took place near the end of the southwestern Indian Wars. Plácida was taken to Mexico by her captors, subsequently escaped, was returned to her family, and told her story to her relatives and her community, Cubero, New Mexico. Her story, later written as a ballad in Spanish and set to music, is the subject of this account.

This author originally heard the story from Arthur G. Bibo. An extremely astute rancher, Bibo knew the vast area of west central New Mexico as if it was his own backyard. He was always willing to share his hard-earned firsthand knowledge about the region around his ranch and the Indian and Hispanic people there. Active with the businesspeople in the Grants, New Mexico, area, he helped establish the Grants Chamber of Commerce and the Lava Soil and Water Conservation District. Arthur was well known in the ranching community in the western part of the state during his lifetime and he always went by the name of Arty, which he spelled with a "y."

Arty was born in Bernalillo, New Mexico, on January 4, 1899. Raised in Cubero, he grew up with families that were direct observers of or defenders in Nana's raid or Romero's abduction and recovery. His father, Emil Bibo, and other uncles, established, owned, and operated general stores and trading posts, at various times, in Cubero as well as in Bernalillo, Laguna, Seboyeta, and Grants. Arty could speak, read, and write Spanish just as well as he could English, along with a smattering of Keresan, the language of the Acoma and Laguna peoples. German was the first language Arty learned since it was spoken by his parents in his childhood years, Spanish was the second, and then English. When he was twelve his family moved to San Francisco, California, for the education of Arty, his older sister, Irma, and his younger brother, Phillip. At the age of eighteen, Arty returned to Cubero to begin his vocation in the cow and ranching business; he owned and operated a small dairy in Cubero at the beginning of his career.

Many descendants of this story's leading characters also worked with Arty later, on his ranch, and became sources of information about Plácida's history. Arty had two major connections with this story that compelled him to begin researching it for posterity. When buying property for his Los Pilares ranch in the 1940s, he acquired the homestead site of Manuelita (a daughter of Plácida) and her husband, Antonio Armijo, and there he built his ranch headquarters. Also, in 1900 the "Corrido de Plácida Romero" was performed as a play, a comedia, with family members and Cubero residents acting the various roles. Arty remembered being told that his father had actually photographed the members of the cast of this reenactment.

I first met Bibo in 1961 at the time when he had stopped active ranching and leased his holdings (about thirty sections) to other area ranchers. He was still active, however, in the ranch realty business, keeping an office in downtown Albuquerque in the old Korber Building on Central Avenue. As a neighbor of Bibo in Albuquerque, I began to help him with his projects at the ranch and with some of his other interests on weekends when I was not working. Arty sold the working portion of his ranch in 1964, keeping his house there and some acreage.

At this time, he became interested in actively researching the life story of Plácida Romero. In about 1965 I started helping him with the family and ballad research. During this period, Arty's health and eyesight began to deteriorate rapidly, and I would drive him when he wanted to go to the ranch house, interview friends about the ballad, or visit former governors from Acoma Pueblo. I also spent many hours in those days at the University of New Mexico's Zimmerman Library, sitting at microfilm readers, researching territorial archives, and gathering information related to the story. Also researched later were the New Mexico Records Center and Archives in Santa Fe and National Archives and Records Administration in Washington, DC.

Arty was well liked at Acoma and had many friends there. One of his uncles, Solomon Bibo, had married into the Acoma people and been elected pueblo governor on three separate occasions. Arty's father Emil was also known to have been a great friend of the Acomas. Nathan Bibo, an older brother of Arty's father, said: "Emil's life and soul were to a great extent devoted to the emancipation of the Acoma Indians, who regarded him as their honest advisor and best friend."[1]

Arty Bibo's ranch bordered the Acoma reservation on the west, his headquarters standing approximately fifteen miles south of Interstate 40 (Route 66 in those days) on NM State Road 117.

In July 1971, when Arty realized he could no longer take care of his ranch house in Los Pilares Valley, I bought his remaining property there. I immediately moved from Albuquerque to the Los Pilares ranch house and even changed my occupation to make a living in the Grants area. In 1972 Arty died of complications from diabetes, which had plagued him most of his life. Some of the best words describing Arty's life and passions were written at that time in a eulogy by another good friend of his, the prominent western historian John L. Kessell, and published in the *New Mexico Historical Review* (see appendix 2).

Rosa Trujillo in 1986 holding a photograph of Plácida (*right*) and her daughter, Manuelita (*left*). This is a three-generation photograph, Rosa being the daughter of Manuelita. Photograph by Miguel Gandert.

Arty was raised very close to the location of the raid and to the family members of Plácida Romero, and had he not taken an early interest, the narrative could not have been recovered in the detail presented here. The story was tape-recorded and transcribed, and that document became the basis of this work. My main contributions to the dictated version were two: finding the locations mentioned in Arty's account and in the ballad and conducting, over many years and many miles, the historical and field research that supports and confirms Plácida's story. I have retained the original place names used for reference and inserted their modern counterparts in parentheses. I have also included many historical connections with this story that have been discovered since the time of its original dictation. It is my intent to provide as complete as possible a historical record of this tragic occurrence. The reader will find many side subjects or subsequent story lines woven throughout that cannot be separated from this text. Some of these story facets would make focal points for additional books or exhaustive studies in themselves. Hopefully some of New Mexico's excellent historians, ethnohistorians, and genealogy scholars will pick up the challenge. This work includes historical sources unknown or overlooked by previous scholars.

As I began helping Arty piece together the story of Plácida Romero, one of our most difficult tasks was to obtain an accurate translation of the ballad. I first saw the original ballad in its handmade cloth cover during an interview between Arty Bibo and Rosa Trujillo (a granddaughter of Plácida) in 1966. This document had always been kept within Plácida's side of the Gallegos/Romero families. The person who most performed the ballad in later years was Rosa's husband, Felipe.[2] At that time, I perused the document and counted the pages and verses. Arty received the original as a gift in 1969. The original ballad was given to me after his death in 1972, and it has been in my possession ever since.[3]

The original transcription of the ballad was handwritten in elaborate orthography in ink with a quill pen circa 1882. Since it wasn't done on high-quality or even good-quality paper, the transcription has faded significantly. Fluent in Spanish, including the local dialects spoken in western New Mexico, Arty had served as a consultant for publications and other endeavors on the usages of early New Mexican Spanish. However, his vision was too poor to attempt the translation—he was

Handmade cloth cover on the original transcription of the Corrido. Photograph by A. E. Roland.

practically blind by this time—so he asked his sister, Irma Belle Bibo Floersheim, who was living in Springer, New Mexico, to help out. She actually did the major work of the translation but could not complete the job, for some words in the original transcription were illegible.

After Arty's death, his wife Nell gave me all the documents relating to Plácida's story that we had collected in the hope I would complete the manuscript and have it published. I knew the translation was incomplete, and although I had the story, it was not, at that point, complete and cogent enough for publication. There were many gaps and uncertainties that, I knew, would take considerable time and research to remedy. With this challenge, I continued to work on getting the ballad properly translated.

Completion of an accurate translation of the ballad was a major step in the process but increases in my job responsibilities and other personal factors prevented me from proceeding with the necessary research on the story to produce a suitable manuscript.

In 2004, after I had retired from the mining industry as an engineer, I effectively began to complete this work. During the interim I had collected many books and other published materials and acquired the knowledge that enabled me to fill the gaps in Romero's story. During my research I also discovered, in a few recently published histories, incorrect assumptions that authors probably would not have made had this material been available at that time. The major incorrect assumption is that the murders of the ranch owner and his partner and the capture of Plácida and her child occurred in the village of Seboyeta, New Mexico, instead of at Rancho Cebolla in Cebolla Canyon. In fact, Nana's raiders were never closer than thirty air miles to Seboyeta, and this information is confirmed in military dispatches. This misunderstanding was apparently promulgated in 1987 and subsequently has been repeated by other historians and in syndicated historical newspaper articles.[4]

The second most daunting task was ascertaining the accuracy of this story. I knew the published timelines that were recorded and sought to substantiate how the pieces of the story fit the episodes established in military and newspaper records. Information on the military activities came mostly from contemporary newspaper articles and military documents. Many area newspapers carried articles about Nana's raid: the *New Mexican* from Santa Fe; *El Progresista* from El Paso del Norte; the *Deming Headlight*; the *Río Grande Republican* from Las Cruces; the *Red River Chronicle* from San Lorenzo, New Mexico; the *Albuquerque Daily Journal*, and *Albuquerque Review;* the *Silver City Miner Chronicle;* and even the *Chicago Times*. Secondary histories on the Buffalo Soldiers in New Mexico shed no new light on the events surrounding Plácida's capture by Nana's raiders.[5]

Nana, Chief of the Warm Spring Apaches. Photograph by Ben Wittick, ca. 1880–90. Palace of the Governors Photo Archives (NMHM/DCA), Ben Wittick Collection, neg. no. 016321.

I did not originally envision tracking the Apache movements to the extent that I have, but for a long time I was puzzled about how Nana's party could pull off the murders at Rancho Cebolla on August 8 and then, just a few hours later, on August 9, raid for horses, and kill and kidnap settlers at Rancho García, a rough sixty trail miles away, while evidence indicated Nana had spent some time at two campsites in between the two ranches. Also, Nana's killing of the New Mexican sheep ranchers/freighters and burning of their ox-drawn wagon in Alamocita Creek had never been accounted for in anything that had been published, nor the victims identified.

These incongruities baffled me for years until the significance of a small newspaper dispatch in the *Albuquerque Daily Journal,* dated August 11, 1881, finally made sense to me. This article stated that Nana's forces had divided, with some men striking targets east of Laguna and some west of McCartys. It suddenly became clear how all these events could transpire almost simultaneously, and that insight enabled me to map the routes that would have been used by the Indians in the areas important to this story. This was a raid of vengeance, in retaliation for the death of the famed Apache chief Victorio almost a year earlier. The actions and motivations of the Apaches are not the focus of my story; I limit this study to the account of Nana's raid, the attack on Cebolla Ranch, the kidnapping of Plácida and her baby daughter, Trinidad, the impact on her family, and the evolution of the ballad. However, the Indian events also established an accurate timeline for Plácida's experiences and, as I was to learn later, this information addressed some other gaps in the historical records about Nana's raid. I was once told by a bona fide historian: "Wow—you are the only person who has been able to decipher Nana's movements and locations north of highway 60 in New Mexico in 1881." Apparently Plácida's story revealed considerable information that had stymied many Southwest historians. Of particular importance is the preservation and interpretation of the "Ballad of Plácida Romero," which is still sung in some variations by her descendants today.

The 1880s was really an interesting time in western Valencia County, New Mexico Territory (now Cíbola County), in particular for the little town of Cubero, the surrounding area of Grants, and the Indians of the Acoma-McCartys region. In the year 1881 the railroad was completed from Albuquerque to Gallup. It wound its way along the valleys of the Río Puerco and Río de San José, passing through the towns of Old Laguna, Acomita, McCartys, Grants Station, as it was called at that time, and Thoreau. It was the extension of the Atlantic and Pacific Railroad, later, in 1897, to become the Atchison, Topeka and Santa Fe. The three Grant brothers (Angus, Lewis, and John) from Canada, who owned a contracting firm, did the main construction at that time building the railroad line through Grants, the town that still bears their name.[6]

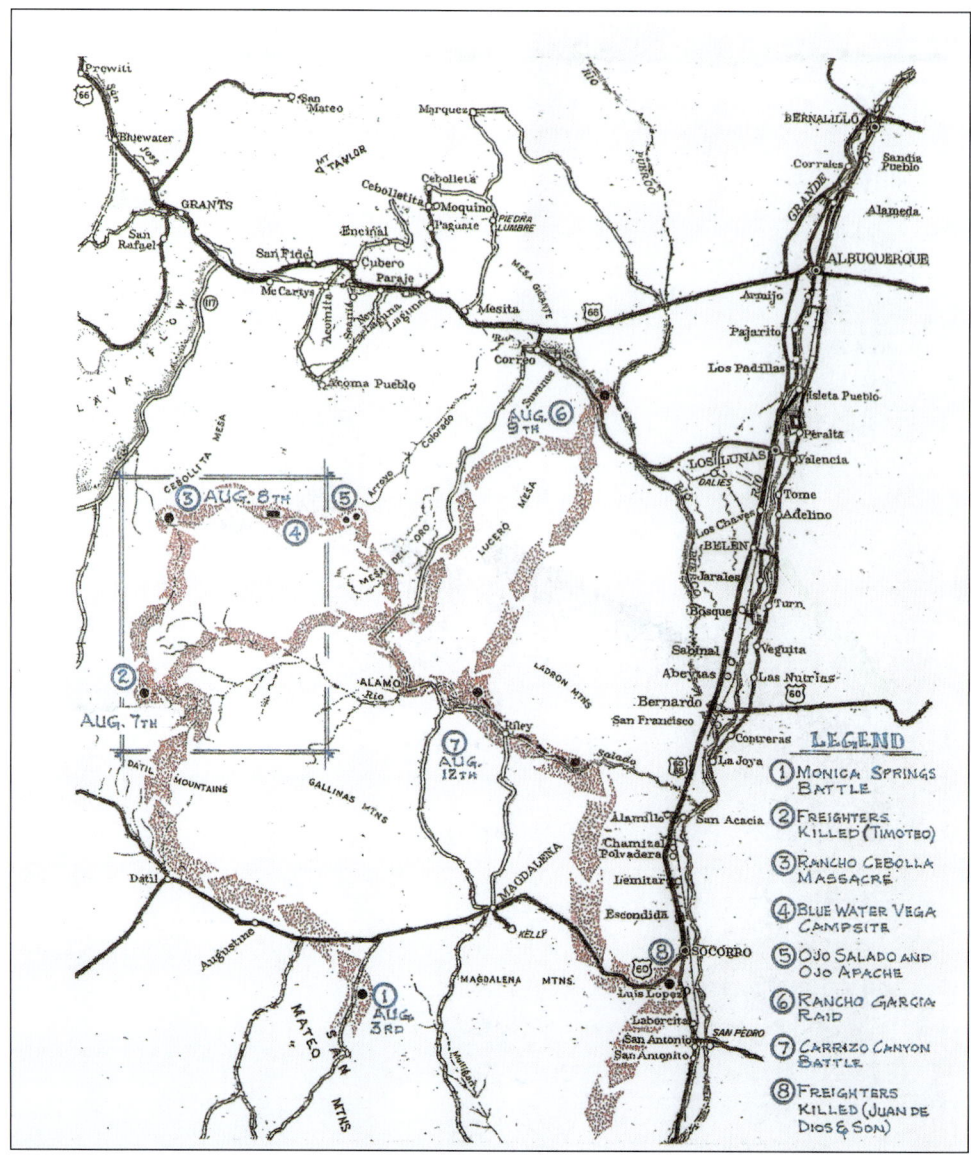

Routes of Nana's forces beginning with the battle at Mónica Springs. Map by A. E. Roland.

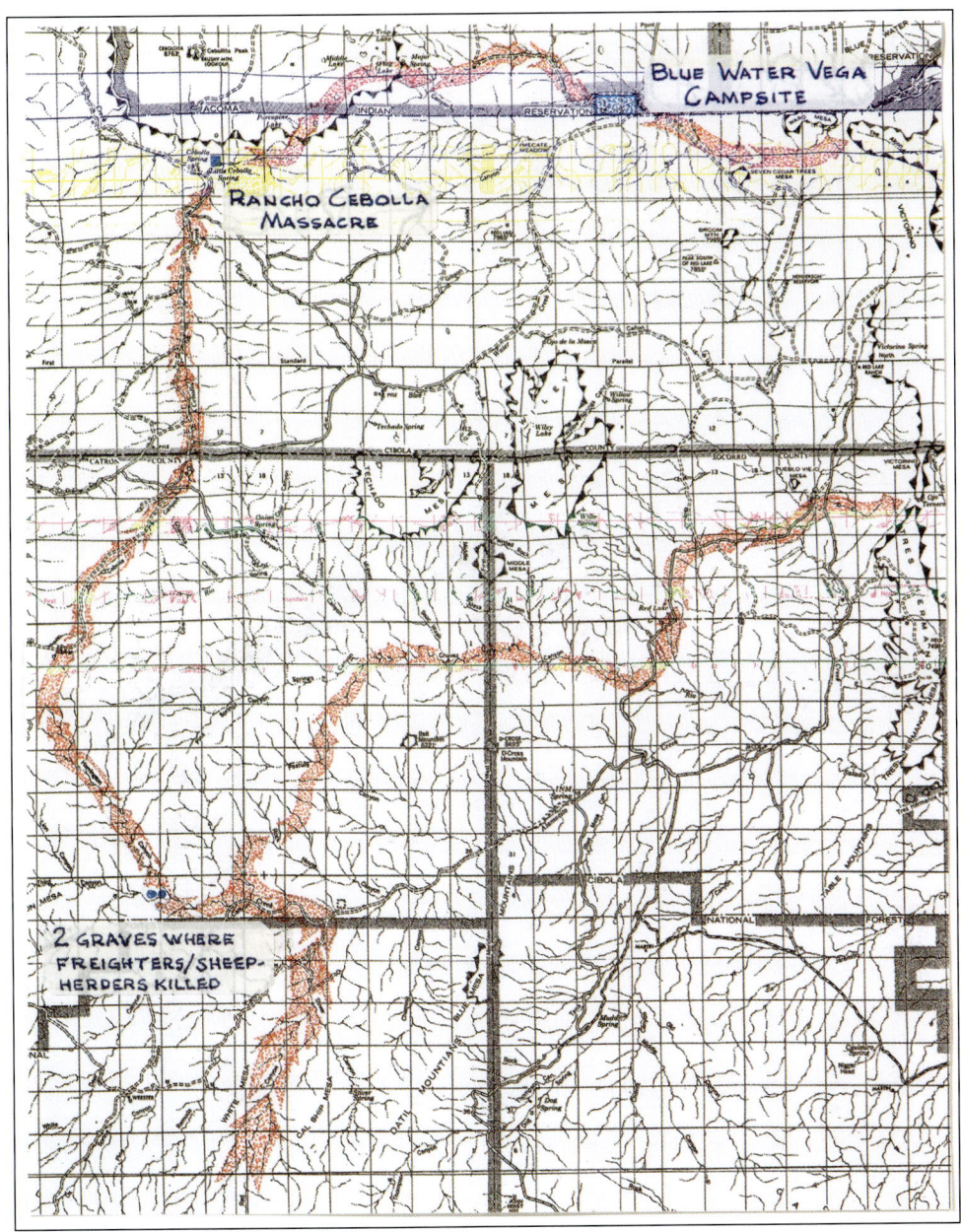

Raider's routes in the vicinity of Rancho Cebolla. Map by A. E. Roland.

The coming of the railroad meant an opportunity for trade, and the first trading post was built in Grants in 1881 by one of Arty's uncles, Simon Bibo. It is possible that the Gallegos family could have done business there.

Also in 1880–82 Adolph Bandelier, the historian and archaeologist, began tramping westward to conduct some archaeological and historical work in the Southwest. In 1882, as he followed the railroad west toward Grants, he investigated to the south and west a short distance from the present village of McCartys. From the east edge of the lava beds (El Malpais National Monument) he went south, following the various Indian ruins that were strung out for some forty miles south of that point. As he reached the place well known as Las Ventanas, eight miles south of I-40 on State Road 117, he not only examined some of the ruins there but mentioned in his journals the beautiful, fertile valley, then lush with grasses and unhurt by drought and overgrazing. Although hidden from the present highway routing, several sandstone windows (*ventanas*) are located here. From Las Ventanas, Bandelier hiked to the head of the Cebollita Valley, where he noted the location of the Ków-ina Spring and the Ków-ina fortified Indian ruin, a place that was inhabited at one time by the Calabash clan of the Acomas, according to Acoma oral history, as was related to Arty by Acoma tribal elders.[7]

In 1881, thirteen miles south of this area, Nana's war party attacked Rancho Cebolla, the home of Plácida Romero Gallegos and her family. The incident was recalled by many newspapers and much discussed for several years. Stories of the event were told even fifteen and twenty years later about the cruel abduction by the Apaches of Plácida Romero during a time when the Apaches were doing a lot of raiding and killing in this part of New Mexico.

Later, in 1942, this story was again told to Arty, and it piqued his curiosity as he was camped in the locale of the occurrences and was consolidating landholdings in this area for his ranch. Having ridden on horseback through the entire country, he recognized and knew all the places related in the story.

After Arty sold the working parts of his ranch in the Cebollita and Los Pilares Valleys, conversations with other people jostled his memory again about this story and the ballad in Spanish about Plácida's abduction. With the cooperation of a number of people in the town of Cubero, Arty began accumulating material on this event, but lacked all the verses that make up the ballad. It was his intention to go to the person who owned the original transcription and obtain a copy, but he was unable to acquire the entire document at that time. Arty left the matter alone for a few years, accumulating whatever material he could in the interim. When I began helping Arty, we were able to find several copies or partial copies from family descendants and musicians who had performed the ballad until, eventually, Arty received the original as a gift. Now the corrido, the newspaper accounts, and the stories of the incident as told by many people have been pieced together again, to save this important and tragic bit of New Mexico history.

It was in the spring of 1942 that Arty trailed a few head of steers from his home ranch at Cubero to the Cebollita Canyon. A close friend and fellow ranch hand, Pablo Brito, accompanied him on this drive and looked after the camp while Arty drove the steers up to the water source (Ków-ina Spring, Acoma name; Cebollita Spring, Spanish name) at the head of the valley. That night around the campfire they reminisced about the individuals from Cubero who had settled and homesteaded in this area and in the Cebolla Canyon, thirteen miles to the south of there, and Pablo retold the story of the murder of the men from Cubero by the Apaches, and the kidnapping of the woman and her child.

Rancho Cebolla at the top of the knoll looking west across the Little Cebolla Spring in the foregound. Photograph by Lee Marmon.

Ruins of Rancho Cebolla looking west. Photograph by Lee Marmon.

2
The Tragic Capture of Plácida Romero

I IMAGINE THE SHEEP DOGS were the first to notice the Indians coming down the valley toward the ranch house and alerted the occupants early, around 6:00 a.m. according to the ballad, on the morning of August 8, 1881. This was a Monday, two days before El Día de San Lorenzo (Saint Lawrence Day, August 10). Just at breakfast time, Domingo Gallegos and his wife Plácida saw the group of Apaches and Navajos, nineteen in number, riding slowly toward their domicile in Cebolla Canyon.[1] The Indians came from the southeast and would have encountered the corrals, stables, and lambing pens that were among the ranch's outbuildings. Passing the corrals and the Little Cebolla Spring, the party rode up a little knoll on which the ranch house was built. As the Indians were approaching the residence, Domingo recognized the Navajos as those who were camped further east, close to what is called Cerro Escoba or Broom Mountain. Observing Navajo custom, the Indians would have dismounted and sat on the ground until they were acknowledged by someone inside the house. The Apaches, of course, followed the lead of the Navajos since they didn't want to raise any suspicions. This morning Domingo probably finished his breakfast before he went out to greet the visitors. He often traded with these Navajos, whom he knew by name.

The previous day Calletano Romero, the elder brother of Plácida Gallegos, who had been visiting his sister, had taken her older child, Manuelita, and the other family children with him back to Cubero to prepare to celebrate the Fiesta de San Lorenzo, the Patron Saint of Cubero. Ironically, the Día de San Lorenzo was also the day on which the great Pueblo Revolt began in the year 1680.

One child, a daughter named Trinidad, remained at home with her parents; she was nine months old then and undoubtedly still nursing. Plácida and Domingo's other children at this time were Felipa, Pedro, Carmel, Vicenta, and Roberto, some of whom stayed with Plácida's parents or other relatives in Cubero. Plácida was twenty-nine years old this summer and, according to family genealogy records and the 1870 census, Domingo would have been thirty-six in 1881. (The 1880 census lists Domingo as being forty; I believe this is an error.[2] A comprehensive list of the children of María Plácida Romero Gallegos is in appendix 3.) Another man, José María Vargas, who worked with Domingo Gallegos and helped take care of the sheep and other ranch livestock, was at the ranch as well. José María was a sheep-ranching partner of Domingo, and they were good companions. The

Rancho Cebolla looking east, the direction from which the Indians approached. Cebolla Canyon turns southeast just in front of the middle mesa. Photograph by Lee Marmon.

Looking into one of the rooms in the bedroom complex at Rancho Cebolla. Photograph by Kelly D. Gatlin.

remaining party at the ranch was also planning to attend the fiesta but had delayed their departure by a day in order to gather and pack some produce to take to Domingo's widowed mother, who lived close to Cubero. The wagon trip to Cubero would have taken one and one-half days, *mas o menos.*

Anna Mae Starr, a grandniece of Plácida, remembered that 1881 was a very wet year in the Cebolla Canyon area, and a great deal of produce had been raised at the ranch. Domingo's mother lived at the settlement known as Los Castillos, a couple of miles northwest of Cubero. The wet condition was also commented on by Captain Parker (Co. K, Ninth Regiment of US Cavalry) who related in a telegram report: "Am water bound and cannot get my [pack] train at Alamosa."[3]

The historical records indicate that Domingo and his partner did not actually own the Cebolla Springs Ranch, but either leased it or worked it on shares, *partidos*, as was common practice in those days.[4] *Los partidos* was a system whereby shepherds could start their own flocks. A larger sheep rancher provided sufficient numbers of ewes and rams and in return he received a percentage of the lamb issue and/or the wool clip until the original value was reimbursed, plus some interest, no doubt. The largest sheep raisers in the area then were French Basque families and the Mirabal family; they could have been the source of Domingo and José María's flock since they resided in the area and in San Rafael, just across the lava beds to the west. (Other renditions of the name José María Vargas have also been encountered in researching this story.[5])

Domingo did not know it at the time, but the headman of this group of Indians was the old Warm Springs Apache leader Nana. Some family sources believe that the party included another well-known renegade by the name of Mangus (son of the past Apache chief Mangas Coloradas).[6] They and Geronimo and Victorio all were giving the US Army a lot of grief in those days, killing and plundering travelers, ranchers, miners, and settlements and taking off to sanctuary in Mexico. Victorio and most of the Warm Springs Apaches had just the previous October been surprised, overtaken, and killed by a Mexican military force at Tres Castillos, a cluster of three granite peaks along the eastern edge of the state of Chihuahua about ninety miles north of Ciudad Chihuahua, Mexico. Nana, an uncle of Victorio, was leading the remnants of Victorio's warriors on this raid of vengeance.

The Rancho Cebolla visitors noticed that Domingo was carrying his pistol this morning, since he was preparing for the trip to the festivities in Cubero, and the Navajos knew him to be a very good shot. After a little conversation in broken Spanish, the Navajos asked him to demonstrate his marksmanship. Domingo thought about this for a while, and decided this would be a fitting gesture to instill in the strangers a due amount of respect. Respect, he knew, was important in Indian cultures, and since he knew the Navajos he did not feel uncomfortable with this request. Domingo then marked a board as a target, set it up on a nearby fence, and proceeded with the demonstration.

All went well, and Domingo impressed the visitors until he had emptied his firearm. Then the strangers shot him once or twice without warning, knocking him to the ground, and while he was helpless one of the Apache raiders picked up a branding iron that was hanging on the fence and hit him on the head. According to the ballad, his brains were scattered over the rocky ground. As they were plundering the premises, some of the invaders dragged Domingo down to the chicken house and threw his body inside. If he was not actually dead, he was injured so severely he could not move. Plácida says in the ballad, "They gave him such a heavy blow with the branding iron that I saw his brains scattered without being able to save him."

Meanwhile, José María was working down at the corrals and lambing pens, about 175 yards east of the house, and was getting the team and wagon ready for the holiday trip to Cubero. I'm sure he would have been looking forward to a joyous time. He most probably had seen the Indians approaching and, also recognizing the Navajos, could have waved or shouted a greeting to them as they passed or possibly as they stopped to water their horses at the spring close to the corrals. When José heard the ruckus and surmised something wasn't right, he grabbed his rifle and started running up the hill toward the ranch house to investigate and help Domingo if necessary. But he didn't make it to the house; the Apaches shot and killed him and left his body where it fell between the house and the corrals. The hostiles immediately ransacked the house, taking what they wanted most, probably some food but mostly money, guns, and ammunition. But that wasn't all they wanted. They forced Plácida to mount a horse and come with them, carrying her baby daughter, Trinidad.

With Plácida captive and Trinidad probably in a shawl arranged as a sling around her mother's shoulders, the Indians left Rancho Cebolla and started back in the direction from which they had come, but going more eastward away from Cebolla Canyon, and climbing a trail up the south slope of Cebollita Mesa. From this higher ledge of rimrock, giving them better defense and surveillance of pursuing army patrols, they headed back into the heavy timber toward the east. This is the area just south of Cerro Montoso or Brushy Mountain (now called Cebollita Peak) and north of Cebolla Canyon.

About this time a detachment of federal troops, lieutenant Francis Guilfoyle with Buffalo Soldier troops of the Ninth Cavalry, who had been following the Indians, were not far from the Cebolla Springs. The soldiers reached the ranch approximately three days later, on August 11, and found the dead bodies of the victims, according to army dispatches, but by then Nana's band had already given the cavalrymen the slip.

The Apaches, with Plácida and her child, paused at the Blue Water Vega (Meadow), at the northwestern base of Cerro Escoba, some twelve trail miles east of where they had murdered Domingo and José María Vargas and fifteen miles due south of Acoma Pueblo. Here the Navajos had a camp by a small spring, and the Apaches made Plácida leave Trinidad with the Navajo families there. Plácida states in her affidavit that the raiding Navajos in that group stayed there also, but the Apaches went on farther east, hauling Plácida along. Of course, Plácida was terrified and heartbroken, as is very apparent in the ballad, but she felt she must not show her feelings lest the Indians kill her too.

Years later, in the 1930s, Arty had the Blue Water Vega country under lease (South ½ of Section 34, Township 6 North, Range 8 West). He said it was a wonderful place to graze cattle and it produced so much grass that one year he was even able to cut and sell some hay.

Ojo (Ojito) Salado with Mesa del Oro in background. Photograph by Lee Marmon.

Ojo Apache closeup. Photograph by Lee Marmon.

3
The Flight to Mexico

Without the burden of the baby, the hostiles knew they would be able to travel much faster when fleeing from the troops. Also, the child would stand very little chance of surviving the rough and perilous trip back to the Apache rancherias in Mexico while the Indians were plundering, murdering, and fighting the Buffalo Soldiers along the way. The Apaches and their captive continued east from the Cerro Escoba country, then went down and through a canyon that was known then, as it is now, as the Alcón, into what is now the Bar 15 Ranch.[1] At that time probably no one occupied this particular spot, which contained a spring known as Ojo (Ojito) Salado and another freshwater spring close by that was later given the name Ojo Apache because these Indians had stopped there with Plácida. An Acoma sheepherder reported to the military that Nana's force was split at this time; some were raiding east of Laguna, and some to the west. Evidence also confirmed that Nana's warriors were involved in a raid at Rancho García (item 6 on the map) on August 9. This would have been only a matter of hours since the murders and kidnapping in Cebolla Canyon on August 8 and some sixty trail miles through rough canyon country to the northeast. Without doubt the Rancho García raiders were the other half of Nana's forces.

Stephen Lekson in *Nana's Raid* reported that six people were killed and 117 horses stolen during this raid, taking his information from Miller, *Nana's Raid of 1881*, and Thrapp, *Dateline Fort Bowie: Charles Fletcher Lummis Reports on an Apache War*. A nine-year-old boy, Procopio García, was also kidnapped from Rancho García at this time.

Portions of the large García family moved to Pueblo del Gallo (present San Rafael, south of Grants) in the early years of that settlement (1870s), from Cebolleta (Seboyeta). They also had a large herd of horses at their ranch, known as Rancho García, on the west banks of the Río San José, close to its confluence with the Río Puerco, about twenty miles northwest of Los Lunas and about twenty miles southeast of Laguna.[2] A large mesa just to the west of this rancho is known to local present-day ranchers as Wild Horse Mesa. The wild horses found there likely escaped during this raid on Rancho García.

The group of Apaches under Nana back at Ojo Apache now departed there with Plácida heading south. They probably climbed the north slope of Mesa del Oro, crossed the top of the mesa, and then went down the south slope to a spring that was known at that location. Mesa del Oro is a long, low mesa with gently sloping sides that is easier to cross over than to go around. John Gunn, an early Valencia County pioneer, identifies and thus corroborates some of the other geographical locations that are part of this history: Ciénega Ranch, forty-five miles south of Laguna; El Rito Valley; the Alcón; and "Seboya" Spring and ranch, about fifteen miles west of the Alcón. Gunn correctly locates Rancho Cebolla and Cebolla Springs although he was just as confused as everyone else as to the directions the Indian raiders were traveling.[3]

From there, Plácida's captors continued south from Mesa del Oro to the valley passing Tres Hermanos ("three brothers"), three peaks close to the Río Salado. Not far from the Río Salado on a rise a little southeast of these peaks was a settlement of mostly peaceful Navajos and Apaches who had lived there and intermarried through the years. Originally known as the Puertecito people (sometimes spelled Puertocito), these people are now known as the Alamo Navajos. The village of Alamo was the probable home of the Navajos who were now guiding and raiding with Nana. A newspaper article of the time reports, "The Navajos at Alamo are believed to be in with the hostiles as they get a share of the plunder."[4]

Considerable confusion is manifest in the names for the Río Salado and Alamocita Creek drainage system, which passes generally west to east through the Alamo Navajo Indian Reservation and continues generally southeast. The Alamocita is a tributary to the Río Salado, and the Río Salado empties into the Río Grande close to San Acacia. Also, all early references as well as present-day local ranchers still call the "Alamocita" watercourse by its original name, the "Alamosa."[5]

The Alamo Navajos were mostly people who had eluded or escaped from Kit Carson's campaign and roundup in 1863–64 and the "long walk" from Canyon de Chelly to Fort Sumner (Bosque Redondo). Some Alamo Navajos were slaves who had escaped their masters from up and down the Río Grande valley and around Socorro. This group of refugees, probably fewer than 150 at that time, also included some Chiricahua and other Western Apaches who preferred living with their Navajo cousins instead of at their reservations at San Carlos or Fort Apache.[6]

Nana's war party went past Puertecito (Alamo) and followed this rough country generally to the east. On August 12 they were forced into an engagement with a pursuing army troop somewhere around the small New Mexican village called Riley today (but not yet established in 1881). This was captain Charles Parker's Co. K, Ninth Cavalry troop of Buffalo Soldiers, at that time stationed "at Alamosa." This battle location northwest of Riley has been described as twenty-five miles west of Sabinal, New Mexico, in military records and close to a canyon named Carrizo or Carrizozo (plural, reeds or ditch grasses).[7] "Carrizozo" is how it appears on modern maps. Harold Miller, in *Nana's Raid of 1881*, surmises from the number of Apaches involved in this fight that the two groups of the Apache forces were reunited at this time. Captain Parker in his telegraphic dispatch describing the results of this battle says "Think hostiles will cross at mouth of Carrizo Creek going east." This would place the actual battle site somewhere slightly northwest of where the Carrizo Creek enters the Río Salado. However, this battle location can be disputed, as we will see. After the engagement Captain Parker's troops retired briefly to the Ciénega Ranch to tend their wounded and send a courier to order food, ammunition, and medical help from Sabinal, New Mexico. They then traveled to the mouth of the Río Puerco to meet the supply train from Sabinal and transfer their casualties. Their route would have been northeastward and probably would have skirted the slopes of Ladrón Peak.[8] Since the season was so wet, they could not get to their own supply packtrain from their Alamosa encampment. The Alamocita and Salado drainages were probably in flood stages, which could have precluded their travel through the Salado Box. From there the troops continued down the Río Grande to Socorro and vicinity to continue their scouting activities.

In the early territorial days, when wagon and teams were the main mode of transportation, travelers going west toward Arizona followed the Río Salado and Alamosa (Alamocita) drainages from the middle Río Grande valley. Today these drainages still have a wide flat bottom and can be traveled for many miles, although they are now heavily eroded, with steep banks and high escarpments. Early settlers have related that in the 1880s these valleys were lush with grasses and contained many *ciénegas* (marshes) that provided wonderful pasturage for teams and camping areas with water and firewood for travelers. Also, when one reached the head of the Alamocita drainage, the country opened up and provided easy accesses going north and south, for instance, north to Fort Wingate or South to Ojo Caliente or the Black Range.[9]

After this battle the Indians headed southeast through the country south of Ladrón Peak and continued south until they crossed the newer wagon road running west from Socorro and through Magdalena. It is apparent the captive victims were kept away from the battle encounters, probably to prevent their escape to, or capture by, the US forces. Plácida would have been in the area of this battle even though she doesn't mention it in the ballad.

When the Indians were fairly close to Socorro—within seven miles—they waylaid a wagon train headed for the Black Range. Later on they came upon Juan de Dios Baca, killing him and his son, Ygnacio. Given that the ballad refers to this incident taking place at the mines close to Socorro, the Bacas might have been miners at work.[10] After pillaging and taking what provisions they wanted out of the wagon train and from the Baca murder site, the Indians took their war south. Plácida says in the ballad that she came upon the Baca murder scene after the killings but, somehow, she could determine the identities of the victims, since they are named in the ballad, or perhaps she learned their names at a later date. The hostiles then continued their raiding frenzy through the Cuchillo Negro and the Black Ranges, killing hapless wayfarers in their path and battling with various troops of the US Cavalry, infantry, and Indian scouts. Finally, they worked their way into Mexico.

4
In Mexico and Return Home

Nana's war party, with Plácida in tow, reached Mexico on August 23, 1881. The stories, as told in the early days by the family, tell of these Apaches taking Plácida to the vicinity of a little Mexican town called Galeana or La Galeana, a village in the valley of the Santa María River about halfway between Casas Grandes and Buenaventura, and within a dozen miles of an Apache stronghold in the foothills of the Sierra Madres in the state of Chihuahua. The Apaches must have entered Mexico not far from Palomas, which lies on the Mexican border south of Columbus, New Mexico. This route agrees with a military telegraphic dispatch reporting that the hostiles had passed, going south, just eight miles west of Fort Cummings (at the southern base of Cookes Peak) on August 21, 1881. The military also picked up the raiders' trail with troops from Ft. Bayard and Ft. Cummings that were reported to be only eight hours behind the hostiles.[1] With the military in hot pursuit, the Indians were making a beeline straight south for the Mexican border and from there they would have continued south, on a trail with many small lakes and rivers to supply them water, to the area of Galeana. This route was known by the military in those days as the Lake Palomas Trail and loosely followed the valley of the Mimbres River, straightening out the large meanders, going south from the western hills of the Black Range, past Cookes Peak and the Florida Mountains and across the border close to present-day Palomas, Mexico.[2]

In this very wet year of 1881 the Mimbres River was probably flowing all the way to the east of Deming, New Mexico, and there would have been water everywhere. In drought years water sources could be few and far between. The Apaches had a winter camp in the area of Galeana, a large rancheria where Nana had left the women and children of the raiding party, according to Plácida. Galeana is close to three other Mexican place names that are mentioned in the ballad: San Buenaventura, a town that grew up around a colonial-era presidio (now known as Buenaventura) on the Santa María River; Sierra Cristo, a mountain northwest of San Buenaventura; and San Joaquín Cañón, located south and west of Galeana.

For some time, I was curious as to whether an Apache rancheria could be identified in the area of San Joaquín Cañón. In the spring of 2008, the opportunity came for an investigation in that country. My guide for this trip was Sr. Luis Benavídez, the tour director for La Tienda Rosa (The Pink Store) in Palomas. San Joaquín Cañón is about ten miles west of the old mining town of Galeana,

Florida Mountains looking south toward Mexico. Nana's escape route would have skirted these mountains. Photograph by A. E. Roland.

Church and plaza at Galeana, Chihuahua, Mexico. San Joaquín Cañón is in the mountain range in the background. Photograph by A. E. Roland.

Chihuahua, Mexico, across the floodplain of the Santa María River, a low, flat area that shows evidence of being very marshy during wet seasons. The canyon proper is narrow, with solid, steep rock walls, allowing excellent defensive and ambushing positions. The southeast side mouth of the canyon widens to provide a very habitable area with flowing or very shallow water, cottonwood trees, and verdant undergrowth amid a thick growth of mesquite trees. The back or northwest end of this canyon is open, providing an easy route for escape.

The presence of a large and apparently long-used Apache rancheria here is evidenced by many six-to-eight-inch-diameter mortar holes in areas of the exposed bedrock as well as stone wickiup foundations, stone corral walls, and oval, cobblestone-lined roasting pits of varying sizes, sometimes called "mescal pits" or "ring middens." There are many broken fragments of metates and manos in the areas of the mortar holes.

This would also be the rancheria where in late December 1845, James Kirker, the "Apache Scalper," known as don Santiago Querque by the Mexican populations, attacked the Apaches west of Galeana. It was reported that, even though the Apaches knew they were coming, Querque and his Indian-fighting crew surprised them and killed many men, women, and children. The governor of the state of Chihuahua, Angel Trías, was paying $200 each for Apache scalps in those days and it was said the scalps were taken to Ciudad Chihuahua and draped over the portal of the Chihuahua City church. A great fiesta ensued.[3]

After the Apaches abandoned this area (probably late in 1881 following Nana's raid), Mexican settlers established a small town of one to two dozen houses utilizing adobe construction and taking advantage of the many stone corrals that had been erected by the Apaches. This village, named San Joaquín, had a modern school and a small church. It appears to have been a viable village for around fifty years but has since been abandoned. The adobe houses are falling into ruin, with the exception of one residence that appears to be occupied, well maintained, and connected to a nearby cattle-ranching operation. A small graveyard and the church receive periodic maintenance, as does a Capilla de los Santos (a little chapel that houses small statues of saints and where passersby can stop and worship) on a small hill overlooking and blessing the area. I believe I have stood at the same spot where Plácida could have been forced to grind mesquite beans or maize at the mortar holes during her captivity.

While holding Plácida captive there the hostile males treated her very badly, and then finally, on September 25, when the whole band was on a raid for more horses, an opportunity for escape became a reality. A newspaper article that first appeared in *El Progresista*, an El Paso del Norte (Juárez, Mexico) newspaper, on October 14, 1881, gives a good basic account of Plácida's escape. The Apache

Wickiup foundation stones at the San Joaquín Rancheria. Photograph by A. E. Roland.

Ring midden/mescal pit at the San Joaquín Rancheria. The mouth of San Joaquín Cañón is visible in the background. Photograph by A. E. Roland.

band was reduced to about twelve warriors by this time and within two hours after their horse raid in the area of San Buenaventura, the Mexican civil authorities with sixty men, led by the chief authority himself, took up the chase. (One wishes the chief authority were named in the article.) According to Plácida, this latest raid was intended to provide horses for Nana's group to go to Chihuahua City to trade their captives for Apaches that had been enslaved there, some of the women and children of Victorio's band captured at the battle at Tres Castillos. Nana held a total of seven captives at this time. The hostile warriors, being pursued by the posse, proceeded in a westward direction where they took defensive positions at Cañón del Cristo. The Mexican authorities skirmished with the Apaches for the rest of the day, over nine hours, but could not drive them from their stronghold. During all of the excitement involving this long battle with the warriors, some of the Apache women, who felt great sympathy for Plácida, helped her and also another captive boy to escape by obtaining a burro for her and giving her some provisions. The captive boy was Procopio García; he and Plácida had become close friends during their captivity. As it turned out, Procopio had been kidnapped by the branch of Nana's group that had raided, killed, and stolen the horses at Rancho García, and they both had undergone horrendous experiences with the murders at Rancho Cebolla, the loss of Plácida's child, and Procopio's family being slaughtered. Plácida and Procopio were soon picked up by the same civil force that was chasing Nana and were taken to the posse's campsite. From that point on, as Plácida related in the ballad, she felt great relief finding herself free and in the hands of Christians. Mexican authorities finally provided them with transportation and an escort to the United States border at Ysleta, Texas, where she and Procopio were provided shelter by a kind family. This apparently occurred prior to October 15 according to a communication from the Mexican Consulate at El Paso to New Mexico's Governor, Lionel Sheldon, and Plácida and Procopio would have been under the custody of the Mexican Consulate. Plácida then began to make arrangements to contact her family in Cubero, by mail, to return with Procopio to New Mexico and home.

The letter and article describing Plácida's escape from Nana's band originally appeared in the newspaper *El Progresista* on October 14, 1881, being sent from Valle de San Buena Ventura [*sic*], Mexico, on September 30, 1881, addressed to Mr. E. Medina, editor of *El Progresista*, and signed by A. P. Mata, a Mexican citizen. The letter was reprinted by the *Santa Fe New Mexican* on October 18, 1881, and then by the Las Cruces *Río Grande Republican* on October 22, 1881. The main purpose of this letter was to alert authorities and the New Mexico territorial government to the presence of these captives in Mexico and elicit help to obtain their freedom and repatriation. This very important letter and article corroborate many items that otherwise would be speculation in this story, although it does misquote Procopio's name as "Probencio." For the full text of these communications, see appendix 4.

In correspondence, Anna Mae relates the abuse of Plácida by the Apaches and how she finally escaped with the help of the Apache women.[4] In the ballad, Plácida laments, "In what travail I've seen myself with these tyrannical Indians," and she was pregnant when she escaped. Plácida was a strong ranch woman who, it was said, could pack mules and horses very well so we assume that the Apache men would have made her work very hard, and raped her.

It would have taken several days or weeks for the mail to get from the area of Ciudad Juárez, Mexico (known as El Paso del Norte in those days), to Cubero, but when it finally did reach there, four men went from Cubero in a wagon to carry Plácida and Procopio home. The return party comprised her brother, Calletano Romero; a cousin, San Juan Romero; a Víctor Romero (unrelated) from Cebolleta; and Petronilo Martínez y Brito, who was the father of Pablo Brito who told Arty this story again in 1942 at Arty's ranch in the Cebollita Valley. We don't know when this repatriation party left Cubero; it could have taken Calletano some time to arrange details and procure a wagon and team.

Apparent in stories from old Cubereños is that, during the long journey home and after going north of Socorro the party took the wagon trail that went west, up the Río Salado watercourse. Leaving the Río Salado east of Alamo the wagon route went north through the future ranch of the Harringtons and the Seis and Wilson holdings (now the Acomas' Bar Fifteen Ranch), and climbed Mesa del Oro. That route continued west through the Red Lake Ranch (also now owned by the Pueblo of Acoma), close to what the old-timers call Victorino Mesa. From there, it angled northwest, then passed Cerro Escoba, where the Apaches and Navajos camped after the killing of Domingo and José María and then proceeded west through Cebolla canyon. Plácida and the others went to Cerro Escoba first to determine if the Navajos were still keeping Plácida's daughter, Trinidad, in the vicinity of the Blue Water Vega, but they were not there. The Navajos had by this time been rounded-up by the military and returned to the reservation. Plácida also wanted to go to Rancho Cebolla to see her husband's and José María's burial accommodations, as would be natural, and possibly to place some wildflowers there.

At least two graves are still visible at the ruin site of Rancho Cebolla. It can be imagined, that after four hot August days and exposure to hungry farm chickens and wildlife predators (coyotes, ravens, turkey vultures, and the like), the bodies of Domingo and José María would have been in horrifyingly bad condition. The burial party covered the bodies with soil and rocks at the places where they were discovered, as was the common practice in remote locations at that time. Probably wooden crosses would also have been erected then, but none remain today.

I first saw the Rancho Cebolla site in the summer of 1970 on a day trip with Arty Bibo. Arty, mostly blind, had expressed the desire to revisit the place since he remembered the ranch ruins and the location from his active ranching days. He wanted to determine how closely the area corresponded to the story as told by the family and to the corrido itself. As I assisted him through the ruin complex and gave verbal descriptions of details Arty couldn't see, we were surprised at how thoroughly we could visualize and reconstruct the story events. Virtually everything dovetailed to present the complete picture of activities on that fateful day. That, of course, was a quick introduction and overview of the area for me. I have since, subsequent to Arty's passing, spent many trips and hours at the site. It took me several years to fully comprehend all the details that I was actually seeing.

At the ruins of the Cebolla Springs Ranch the chicken house can still be identified. In one corner of the chicken house ruin stands an unusually high mound of rocks that was clearly placed there purposely. This is the apparent burial location of Domingo Gallegos. Another obvious gravesite not far away, also under rocks at a location corresponding with the story, would be that of José María Vargas.

As the story went, Domingo was killed close to the house after participating in a brief target shooting episode and his body then was dragged and thrown into the chicken house sixty to seventy yards away, downwind, to the east. About thirty feet from what appears to be the main kitchen door of the rancho is an oval ring of stones, obviously having been there for many decades. This stone arrangement is the size of a man on the ground in a fetal position. There is no explanation for the existence of this ring other than as a monument to mark the location where Domingo was fatally wounded. This testimonial arrangement must have been placed there by Plácida, or by her direction, since she is the only one who would have known that precise location. Plácida's affidavit indicates her return to Cubero was in early April 1882, eight months after the murders and her abduction.

In addition, on a subsequent visit to the ranch site after a rainy season, I discovered a short pistol cartridge casing next to this ring of stones. When I had the casing examined by a gunsmith, I was informed it was .50-caliber center-fire of a make in common use by the military in those days, also commonly stolen and used by the Apaches. This was probably one of the rounds fired by the Indians and even could be the round that mortally wounded Domingo. The casing was photographed in situ and later returned to its original location and buried there.

Apparent upon close examination of this site is that the Rancho Cebolla was effectively abandoned after this massacre. Recent evidence to this effect came from Buddy Major.[5] The Major family settled not far from Rancho Cebolla near the top of Cebollita Mesa (then known as Putney Mesa and now part of the Acoma reservation) at Major Spring and subsequently became large-scale ranchers and landowners in this area. Buddy Major indicated that his family came there in 1916, and he is certain that no one inhabited the Cebolla Springs Ranch buildings at that time or thereafter. There is a more recently built corral in the area of the springs that is still used by local ranchers on a seasonal basis. After the ranch was abandoned the Cebolla Springs were claimed by the nearby Bodenheimer Ranch (also spelled Bodenhamer and Bodenhammer). The ranch, sold and bought several times, became the Mertz Ranch, and later was bought by Buddy Major, becoming known as the Mertz/Major Ranch. Major, now deceased, sold the ranch, which is presently being operated by new owners. The Cebolla Springs and the Cebolla Springs Ranch site have recently been purchased by the Bureau of Land Management and are included in the El Malpais National Conservation Area. The Rancho Cebolla ruins are fenced for protection from grazing cattle.

From Rancho Cebolla the wagon route went on west to the lava beds (El Malpaís) and north through the future and former Bibo Ranch at the Cebollita and Los Pilares valleys (purchased by Acoma Pueblo in 1973), and reached the old wagon road to Cubero near McCartys. As Plácida and her entourage in the wagon neared Cubero at Los Cerritos, where in later years Arty's brother, Phillip, had a store/trading post and ranch (presently the site of Acoma's Sky City Casino), they were greeted by a large group of friends and relatives from Cubero who had heard their arrival was imminent.

After she returned home, Plácida told her story in Cubero, and a woman named María Gutiérrez put it into verse and song. The ballad was not written down immediately but was passed on verbally for some time. Eventually another man, Melquiades Otero, from Rinconada (now known as San Fidel) in the Cubero region, who was well educated in Spanish, took down the words in longhand on lined paper similar to what used to be in a Big Chief Tablet. This ballad related quite an adventure, and Plácida's story—how she was lucky enough to escape her captivity and return home—became the talk of the town.

5
The Military Pursuit

I𝐍 1882, 𝐀 𝐘𝐄𝐀𝐑 𝐀𝐅𝐓𝐄𝐑 N𝐀𝐍𝐀'𝐒 𝐑𝐀𝐈𝐃, the US War Department summarized the United States portions of this raid: "In July, 'Nana,' with fifteen warriors, the remnant of 'Victoria's' [*sic*] band, re-entered New Mexico, and, re-enforced by about twenty-five Mescaleros, whirled through the territory, plundering and killing a number of people. On the 17th of July, at Alamo Canyon, New Mexico [close to present day Alamogordo, New Mexico], a small party of these Indians ambushed Chief packer Burgess and one man, belonging to a detachment commanded by Lieutenant Guilfoyle, Ninth Cavalry, wounded Burgess and captured three mules."[1] This was John Francis Guilfoyle from Maryland. He was appointed to the US Military Academy from Maryland and graduated fortieth in the class of 1876—2nd lieutenant, 9th Cavalry, June 15, 1877; 1st lieutenant, Ninth Cavalry, November 1, 1881; and breveted 1st lieutenant for gallantry against Indians at White Sands, July 19, 1881, at San Andres Mountains, July 25, 1881, and at Mónica Springs, August 3, 1881.[2]

> On July 19, Lieutenant Guilfoyle, with his detachment of the Ninth Cavalry and some Indian scouts, following a trail westward of Cañon del Perro [Dog Canyon], New Mexico, had a skirmish with some of the hostiles near the Arena Blanca [White Sands], where they had just killed two Mexicans and a woman; the party numbered about thirteen warriors, and succeeded in making their escape. On July 26, Lieutenant Guilfoyle again struck the hostiles encamped in the San Andres Mountains, New Mexico, captured two horses, twelve mules, many blankets, and all the Indians' provisions; two of the hostiles were shot and believed to be killed; the others escaped, crossing the Río Grande six miles below San José, killing two miners and a Mexican in the flight. [San José was a small settlement close to present-day Elephant Butte Dam. The site is now covered by the lake.]
>
> July 30, four Mexicans were reported killed by the hostiles in the foothills of the San Mateo Mountains.[3]

Some correspondence from a woman who described herself as the wife of a descendant of a sister of Plácida indicates that a brother of her grandmother was one of these persons killed here during the Nana raid while herding the family sheep. The family is from the area of Belén, and their stories tell us that these killings took place in or near East Red Canyon in the San Mateos in late July 1881.[4] This is very interesting information, but there is some confusion here. Plácida did have an older sister by the name of Josefita. However, the only trace of her ever recovered has been a birth certificate; otherwise, she is absent from genealogical sources. Some family members surmise that she died in infancy. This is a mystery.

"August 1, a party of thirty-six citizens, commanded by a Mr. Mitchell, whilst at dinner in the Red Canyon of the San Mateo Mountains, were surprised and defeated by the hostiles, losing one man killed and seven wounded, besides all their riding animals, thirty-eight in number; the Indians escaped. On August 3, Lieutenant Guilfoyle's detachment again struck this band at Mónica Springs, New Mexico, wounded two Indians and captured eleven head of stock, some saddles, blankets, &c."[5]

This is the same Mónica Spring, at the extreme north end of the San Mateo Mountains, where in the fall of 1863 Manuel Antonio Chávez, hero of the Civil War in New Mexico for guiding major John Chivington's Colorado Volunteers onto the supply trains of Sibley's Confederates and their subsequent destruction, had what he called the greatest fight of his life. Here, with about a dozen men during a two-day battle, he held off more than a hundred Navajo raiders who were stealing sheep in the Río Grande valley. Although only three of his party survived the ordeal, the Navajos were routed, with many being killed, and the sheep were recovered.[6] The War Department summary continues, "this band [in 1881] numbered about twenty or thirty warriors, led by Nana, and they had killed another Mexican in escaping from Red Canyon [in the Dátil Mountains]. **At La Savoya [Cebolla], New Mexico, on August 11, Lieutenant Guilfoyle found that two Mexicans had been killed and two women carried off by the hostiles.**"[7]

Dan L. Thrapp's *Dateline Fort Bowie* places the Mitchell encounter at Red Rock Canyon.[8] This would distinguish the location from West Red Canyon or East Red Canyon, which are also in the southern half of the San Mateo Mountains. However, a military communiqué reports that the Mitchell party left Nogal Springs (in Nogal Canyon on the east side of the San Mateos) tracking the Indians ten miles north to the mouth of Red Canyon, where the ambush occurred.[9] This description indicates the location would have been the East Red Canyon of the San Mateos and is probably the most credible. Lummis also relates that Nana's band had a sixteen-mile running battle with the troops when leaving Mónica Springs and that Nana escaped through the Dothill (Dátil) Mountains and killed several Hispanos on the way. This information is reported to have come from Frank Bennett, who at that time was Lieutenant Guilfoyle's chief of scouts. The Dátil Mountains basically run east-west with two south-north passes transecting them: Davenport Canyon lies on the west end and Red Canyon on the east end. Both passes disgorge into the Alamocita Creek drainage area on the Dátils' north side, an extremely rough, remote, and canyon-riddled country that is even today difficult to access and travel. This route would have taken Nana through the Red Canyon in the Dátils. This mostly narrow flat-bottomed canyon starts at the Blue Springs area near the top of the Dátil Mountains, runs down the Dátils' north slope and then joins the Alamocita. It was often used as a shortcut by horseback travelers and as a route to drive cattle and sheep through the eastern end of the Dátils. Not far from the mouth of the Red Canyon, going west along the Alamocita, two graves are still visible today where early Dátil country ranchers and homesteaders recall that two New Mexican sheep ranchers, who were freighting supplies back to their ranch near Rito Quemado, New Mexico, were killed and their ox-drawn wagon burned during the time of Nana's raid. This occurrence is featured in Agnes Morley Cleaveland's memoir *No Life for a Lady* and is where the famous ox-chain was found that is also part of her story.[10] This murder site is only seventeen straight-line miles (twenty trail miles) south of the Rancho Cebolla murder site.

The freighters were traveling west along the Alamocita, and when Nana's band came into the Alamocita from Red Canyon, the Indian lookouts or outriders likely saw the fresh wagon and oxen tracks. Here Nana may have divided his forces, leading one group to plunder the wagon, which was three or four miles to the west, and then to travel north to Rancho Cebolla for possible guns and ammunition there as well, the other group to ride northeast to Rancho García, which was known by the Navajos for raising horses. Eve Ball, in *Indeh*, reports: "Nana—his power was over ammunition trains and rattlesnakes. Victorio's Bravest, such as Kaytennae, might make a raid for bullets and fail. But when Nana, long past eighty and crippled, rode all night, he brought back ammunition."[11] These locations were well known to the Navajos who were raiding with Nana.

Further research into the grave sites of the two New Mexican freighters (number 2 on the overall routes map), and an interview with a present-day relative of the Baca family[12] indicate that one of the graves at this site is probably that of Timoteo Baca, the other probably being that of Ignacio Baca, who was killed here during Nana's raid according to Espinosa and Chávez in *El Río Abajo* (see chapter 3, note 10, this volume). This source also states the date was August 7, 1881, although this may have been the day the remains were found, with the actual killings occurring a day or two earlier since we know Nana was at Rancho Cebolla early in the morning on August 8. At least three men were in this freighting party, two of whom were killed here on the Alamocita. One member of the group, Ramón García, escaped on foot, until he could obtain a horse, and hid from the pursuing Indian raiders, and because he escaped, the knowledge of this bit of history has survived. As the story goes, he didn't stop running from the gut-wrenching murder site until he got into Colorado. Along the way, as the Indians looked for him in the cliffs and rocky places, his sheep dog kept growling and barking whenever they got too close. Because of this, Ramón had to kill his dog by smashing its head with a rock to keep it from giving away his hiding places and this necessity was said to have been very upsetting to Ramón. Later, after the Indian raiders were subdued, he returned to the Quemado area and continued to raise sheep there for many years.

The murder of Timoteo Baca subsequently became known to relatives of his around Belén, and became the subject of another New Mexican ballad, "El Corrido de Timoteo Baca." The composer, who was not an eyewitness to this event, introduced many factual errors in the corrido. The main goal of this rendering appears to have been to commemorate Timoteo Baca, as would be expected and natural at a funeral ceremony. N. G. Baca knew Ramón García in his early years, had been told the story of the murders by Ramón, and believes Ramón García died in the 1940s. This interview with Sr. Baca also established, from reports received from shepherds who had flocks in the Alamocita country, that Alamocita was as far west as Nana's party ventured at this time. From here the group led by Nana would have been guided northward by the Navajos, traveling up the meandering trail through Harrington Canyon, the most direct route into the Cebolla Canyon and to Rancho Cebolla. Probably no more than one or two warriors made a brief search for Ramón García. The other half of Nana's raiding force went northeast for the horses at Rancho García.

The War Department summary and current newspaper dispatches state Lieutenant Guilfoyle's detachment arrived at the Cebolla Springs Ranch on the evening of August 11. The troopers found two men had been killed and two women had been carried off, according to the *Albuquerque Daily Journal*, August 12, 1881. This important information indicates that members of Plácida's and Domingo's family became concerned when they did not show up in Cubero on August 9 as was planned, and they had sent a party on horseback to help or to find out what happened. This party, according to family sources, comprised Plácida's brother, Calletano, and several well-armed citizens who were certainly aware of the hostile activities in the area by this time. The Cubero search party could have been in the process of burying the remains at Rancho Cebolla at the time the troopers arrived on the scene. In any case, there had to be communications between family or friends and the federal troops in order for the army to know at this time that, in addition to the two dead men at the site, two females had also been abducted.

The War Department summary states, "August 12, Captain Parker, with a detachment of nineteen men of the Ninth Cavalry, struck Nana's band twenty-five miles west of Sabinal, New Mexico; lost one soldier killed, three wounded, and one missing, but reported an equal loss inflicted upon the hostiles, who then drew off; Captain Parker's small detachment, encumbered by their wounded, were unable to pursue." This is the site known as the Battle of Carrizo Canyon or the Battle of Ciénega Ranch in military records. Plácida does not mention this occurrence and may not have witnessed it. Actually, two troopers were killed in this combat; farrier Guy Temple and private Charles Perry.[13] After this engagement Captain Parker fell back to Ciénega Ranch to tend the wounded soldiers and arrange for needed supplies and ammunition. One aspect of this fight that has not been examined to date is the location of the Ciénega Ranch; however, there is a very old ranching establishment in this vicinity shown on some old maps as Rancho de los Chávez. It was a sheep ranch begun in 1872 by José Angel Chávez and is close to Carrizo Canyon and about eleven miles east of Alamo. Locally known as the Angelita Ranch, it was the only ranch in that area in 1881 and is undoubtedly the location of Captain Parker's layover. This is also the area of the Río Salado known as La Ciénega (the marsh) and where Cañon de la Ciénega enters the Río Salado from the north. I surmise that the area of the mouth of Ciénega Canyon was the place where Captain Parker's scouts picked up the trail of Nana's hostile party and where, shortly before, another raid had taken place on the wagon train of Solomon Barth, a trader from St. Johns, Arizona, who survived the raid. Another man, a companion of Barth, was also killed. This event may have been perpetrated by the other segment of Nana's group that had raided Rancho García. If so, Plácida was likely unaware of it at that time. At any rate, the troops were again hot on the hostiles' trail. I also believe, had not Parker's troops been patrolling the area, this ranch by the Ciénega would have been the raider's next target for massacre and plunder, being guided that way by the Navajos from Alamo. These Navajos held a strong dislike for this rancher. The land status here today is partially BLM and New Mexico trust lands leased to area ranchers. There is another apparent battle site approximately twenty miles southeast along the Río Salado containing two graves that some historians believe to be the actual battle site where Parker's troops caught up with the renegades. The military dispatches and later reports are extremely unclear on this location. ¿Quién sabe?, the jury is still out. This site is contained within private ranch land with restricted access.

> August 16, Lieutenant Valois, with Troop I, Ninth Cavalry, had a severe fight with a band of about fifty Indians, near Cuchillo Negro, New Mexico; Lieutenant Burnett, Ninth Cavalry, was wounded twice, two enlisted men and six horses were killed; the hostiles lost several killed. The same day Lieutenant Taylor, with a detachment of the Ninth Cavalry, also had

a fight with the hostiles, captured some horses and recovered some stolen property, losing, himself, a few horses killed; the hostiles were pursued toward the Black Range.

August 18, Lieutenant G. W. Smith, Ninth Cavalry, with a detachment of twenty men, struck the hostiles about fifteen miles from McEver's ranch, New Mexico [present-day Lake Valley, New Mexico]. The Indians were defeated after a very severe fight, in which Lieutenant Smith and four of his men were killed; a party of citizens, under command of George Daly, joined Lieutenant Smith in the fight, and Daly was killed [also known as the battle of Gavilan Canyon and, obviously, the Indians were not defeated].

Altogether, eight troops of cavalry, eight companies of infantry, and two [companies of] Indian scouts were in the field, personally commanded by Col. E. Hatch, Ninth Cavalry, in pursuit of these Indians, and while no decisive engagement took place, the hostiles were persistently driven from one point to another, until they fled across the Mexican border, where, under positive orders from the government, the chase was abandoned.[14]

From these War Department descriptions, it is easy to envision why the nine-month-old girl, Trinidad, even with the care of her mother, would have a slim chance of survival traveling hundreds of miles between Cebolla Canyon and deep into the state of Chihuahua, Mexico, on foot and on horseback and through several brutal fighting campaigns.

6
The Aftermath

PLÁCIDA HAD BECOME PREGNANT during her captivity in Mexico, and all family sources indicate that shortly after Plácida returned to Cubero she married Victor Romero, from Cebolleta, who was one of the party that brought her back in the wagon from the Mexico border. For that reason, or possibly because Romero was also her maiden name, they refer to her as Plácida Romero although her name was Gallegos at the time her husband was killed. About two months before this time some legislation related to Plácida's return had been considered by the territorial government. The *1882 Acts of the Legislative Assembly of the Territory of New Mexico, Twenty-fifth Session*, reports an act was passed authorizing the Territory to pay for the expenses incurred by persons in obtaining Plácida and Procopio's release and return trip to Cubero. This act was approved January 28, 1882 (see appendix 5) and was probably a response to the previously described letter published first in El Paso del Norte and later in Santa Fe and Las Cruces, as well as entreaties by Plácida's family. Among other inaccuracies, including the date of the Indian attack, it states that Procopio García was an adopted son of Plácida and Domingo. His adoption was not indicated through any family sources, and he was not included in the Gallegos family in the 1880 or 1885 Valencia County Censuses. According to Rosa Trujillo, Procopio was actually a nephew of Domingo.[1] It is probable that Procopio's parents were killed during Nana's raid at Rancho García (six killings were reported there).

In persistent search for Plácida's experiences after her return from captivity, I sought official documentation of her family after the 1880 Census. I discovered nothing exists of the 1890 census, which was destroyed in a fire. However, I became aware of a special Valencia County Census of 1885.[2] In the Cubero listings I could not find Plácida. In going through the entire county census, I finally found her and her family enumerated in the village of La Vega. I was not familiar with that town name in Valencia County, but Julyan's *Place Names of New Mexico* states that La Vega de San José is now known as San Fidel, and it is not far from Cubero. By this time Plácida had a new daughter from her captivity pregnancy listed as Trinidad, the same name as Plácida's kidnapped daughter. This child was listed as two years old, although the census mistook her for a boy, and Plácida was listed as still being a widow. According to church records, Plácida and Víctor Romero did not marry until January 14, 1886, almost four years after her return, and by 1900 they were back in the Cubero area.[3]

Also, at this time in 1882, Adolph Bandelier was staying at Cubero during his western travels and investigations and he mentioned he had visited with Plácida and "conversed with her awhile." He had probably read some of the newspaper articles about her. He described her as being pleasant, young, very resolute, and rather pretty. Bandelier stated his conversation with Plácida took place on May 27, 1882, and the passage also indicates he was a little bit skeptical of her story. He states, "Her story strikes me as doubtful in some points." Plácida possibly overplayed the role of redeemed captive in order to elicit more sympathy for her effort to recover her daughter from the Navajos. In addition, some of the press was unsympathetic to her quarrel with the government Indian agent. She was even accused of lying because her efforts to recover Trinidad were exposing the agent's misconduct in office.

In Bandelier's notes from June 11, 1882, he also relates he met a man named Mónico González from San Marcial who claimed that the same Apache that killed Plácida Romero's husband also murdered his mother, son, daughter, and nephew. No date or location was given for these killings; however, the War Department summary of 1882 places the Nana party in the eastern foothills of the San Mateo Mountains (not far from San Marcial) on July 30, 1881, where they killed four people.[4]

The most important thing to Plácida after escaping captivity was to retrieve her daughter, Trinidad, from the Navajos. A few people at Cubero who were literate, most notably the local notary and justice of the peace, Gregorio Otero, helped her contact the New Mexico territorial governor in Santa Fe and the federal Indian agent at Fort Defiance, Arizona. At that time the Indian Agent, Galen Eastman, was in a lot of trouble for graft and corruption. To say the Navajos were upset with him, calling him by the nickname of "ten-tongued Eastman," is an understatement. However, he insisted on taking their side and made little effort to assist Plácida's recovery of her child. New Mexico territorial governor Lionel Sheldon did all he could for her, but he was powerless in this case because the Navajos were administered by the Bureau of Indian Affairs, a federal agency. By rebuffing Plácida's appeal, Agent Eastman was obviously seeking the favor of the Navajos whose rations he was apparently pilfering for his own profit. Even though Plácida had filed an affidavit, his word carried more weight than hers, and no help was extended from the federal government.

THE AFFIDAVIT OF PLÁCIDA ROMERO

Plácida Romero of Cubero, Valencia County, Territory of New Mexico, being duly sworn in according to law, under oath declares and states that she is the widow of the deceased Domingo Gallegos, who was assassinated on the 8th of August 1881, by Indians, on his Cebolla Ranch in the aforementioned county; that she having been made captive was taken to the state of Chihuahua, Republic of Mexico and there, having escaped from the Indians, she fell into the hands of Mexican authorities, where she remained until her return to New Mexico in April 1882. She says that on the 8th of August, 1881, a party of Indians, 7 Apaches and 12 Navajos, most of the latter well known to her, arrived at her husband's ranch and, after having eaten, the Indians challenged her said husband to shoot at a target with them, and that when they'd finished and the Indians were ready to leave, they shot her husband in the shoulder killing him instantly. That her husband was hit twice, once by the Navajo named Cibusle and second by an Apache. That among the Navajos were many she knew well, among them Cibusle, Margarito, Guero, Chino and others. That immediately after killing her husband, the Indians also killed her husband's companion, one named José María, and that they took her and her 9 month old baby girl captive and took them to a place called Blue Water, close to the Pueblo of Acoma where the Apaches and Navajos separated, the Apaches taking her, and the Navajos her baby girl Trinidad. That the Navajo who took and has her daughter is called Margarito. She says furthermore that she swears this statement with the direct purpose of begging the government of the U.S. to force the return of her daughter and that the assassins of her husband be punished according to the law.

> Plácida Romero.
> Sworn and signed before me this 18th
> day of April 1882.
> Gregorio N. Otero,
> Justice of the Peace.[5]

Some other sympathetic people wrote letters to the press, especially around the Las Vegas, New Mexico, area, critical of Eastman's unresponsiveness in this matter. The newspaper *Crónica del Río Colorado (Red River Chronicle)* particularly blasted Eastman's position. On May 6, 1882, it reported in an editorial that Plácida had presented, in an affidavit, the names of the Navajos who retained her daughter, Trinidad, and begged US district attorney Sidney A. Barnes to move against the Indians in that matter. On June 24, 1882, the newspaper fired another salvo, arguing that Eastman was denying the facts of Plácida's case and calling for a formal investigation by the proper federal authorities. The editor accused Eastman of falsifying his reports about how many Navajos were off the reservation and of stealing the rations of the absent Indians. The *Red River Chronicle* editor suggested that the citizens of Valencia County take matters in their own hands by arresting Agent Eastman and he be "tied to a stake, cut off limb after limb, and roasting his dirty heart in his own body over a slow fire of green wood." He also urged documentation of Eastman's criminal activities be sent to federal authorities, that he be punished, and Plácida's child be returned. On August 9, 1882, the newspaper surmised eight thousand Navajos were off the reservation at that time and Eastman was daily stealing that many rations (see appendix 6).

As the *Red River Chronicle* published these accounts, Plácida was still making attempts to get her child back but ultimately to no avail. According to family sources, her brother, Calletano, aided by friends and family members, finally found his niece years later. By this time, she had been raised as a Navajo, was married, and had a family of her own. Trinidad did not know of her natural parents until repatriation was impractical and probably impossible, and she elected to remain with her Navajo family.

In the ballad, Plácida describes vividly what happened, where they took her the first night or two, and how they had eluded the army. But newspaper accounts that came out when the army officers had gotten word to McCartys, a few days after the massacre, show even more clearly how great the deception had been. One account mentioned that the officers, finding the men dead, sent some couriers on horseback over to McCartys, where they knew there would be a telegraph operator, since the railroad had just been built as far as Gallup that year. The soldiers going to McCartys were not familiar with this country and had to follow Cebolla Canyon west to the lava beds and then on north through the future Bibo Ranch. When the wire reports came into Albuquerque, the sheriff wired Gallup to have some troops from Fort Wingate come toward Grants and see if they could capture these renegades. It was the opinion of everyone that the Apaches were headed with Plácida toward Grants and then northward into Navajo country toward Rincón Marcos, a Navajo settlement some twenty miles northwest of Cabezón Peak.

The next day's article mentions the soldiers were approaching the Grants area, and the Marmon brothers, who had a company of Indian scouts at Laguna, had been alerted. They felt it was just a matter of hours before they would have these Apaches surrounded. What they didn't know was that the Apaches had eluded them and were now going south toward Mexico. There is no evidence the Apache raiders went any farther north than Rancho García, and the established timelines do not allow for further raiding in that direction. In addition, there is a telegraphic dispatch stating the closest the raiders came to El Rito, New Mexico (close to present day Mesita at Laguna Pueblo), was twenty-five miles south.[6] That would have been at Rancho García.[7] It was not until the Indians had had other engagements with the cavalry, near Ladrón Peak and at Cuchillo Negro some days later, that the military discovered they were on the wrong track. All this confusion can be attributed to Nana splitting his forces, whereby different killings and attacks could take place almost simultaneously at widely spaced locations. The *Albuquerque Daily Journal* printed periodic dispatches at this time reporting on the developments as they occurred (see appendix 7).

Plácida's second daughter out of seven children when her husband was killed was named Manuela but was called Manuelita by her family. Manuelita later married Antonio Armijo, and they homesteaded land in the Cebollita Valley and 260 acres in what is called Los Pilares Valley, the next valley to the south. In 1942, Arty Bibo purchased the 260 acres in Los Pilares Valley that Manuelita had sold to a French Basque who ran large herds of sheep in that area. When Arty sold his ranch in 1964 he kept 38 acres of this land not only because that is where he built his ranch headquarters but also because it was the spot on which Manuelita and her husband had homesteaded and raised their family. An archaeological survey report on the Armijo homestead site is included in appendix 8.

Rosa Trujillo was one of their daughters. In 1970, Rosa was seventy-three years old. She is now buried in the campo santo at San Fidel, New Mexico, as is her mother, Manuela. Rosa was born December 1, 1897, and died March 5, 1989, making her ninety-two when she died. Rosa gave Arty not only the original transcription of the ballad, but an item that Domingo Gallegos used to carry with him out in the mountain country as most men did at this time: a pocket-style folding knife that also contained a fork, spoon, screwdriver, and a little saw. She also gave him a little jewelry box that had belonged to Plácida. According to Rosa, Plácida made a promise to Señora de la Luz that if she survived and returned home safely, she would act the entire story of her adventures; the killing of her husband, her abduction, and the loss of her daughter, with the help of the people of Cubero and her family. This she did in about the year 1900, with Rosa playing the part of the baby girl, Trinidad. Rosa was about three years old at the time and it so happened Emil Bibo made a photograph of the entire company taking part in the performance of the ballad story. Unfortunately, many hundreds of Emil's photographs (glass plate negatives) of territorial life and times around Laguna, Acoma, Cubero, Zuni, and Hopi were inadvertently destroyed after his death in 1925. Maybe someone from Cubero still has a copy of that reenactment cast photograph.

During interviews with family members, the date of Plácida's passing could not be positively determined, but Rosa thought she was about twelve when her grandmother died. Plácida was said to have been buried at the Campo Santo Viejo de Cubero. Initial searching did not provide her burial location although several unmarked headstones are present. If Rosa truly was twelve, then Plácida would

Jewelry box that belonged to Plácida given to Arty Bibo by Rosa Trujillo (photograph in author's collection).

have died around 1909 at the age of fifty-seven or fifty-eight. However, there is another clue to this uncertainty. I discovered in church records that her husband, Victor Romero, was remarried on October 6, 1902, to Angelita García, a resident of the village of Juan Tafoya, and they were listed as still being married in the 1910 Cubero census.[8] Since divorces were unheard of in the Catholic Church in those days, and since widowed men had a tendency to remarry not long after the death of a spouse, this most likely was the year of Plácida's death, with her age being closer to fifty. Plácida had to have been a very strong and courageous woman although family members related that her experiences left profound emotional scars. After her return it was said Plácida would cry for days and days, that she was extremely saddened and prayed constantly in many churches, particularly her home church at Cubero, for the return of her daughter.

During the search for Plácida's grave every stone and marker in the old campo santo was examined minutely. One well-maintained gravesite is marked with the name Policarpio Romero, one of the sons of Plácida's brother, Calletano. Some present-day descendants say that Plácida is buried in the stone-mounded but otherwise unmarked grave immediately north of Policarpio's. Also found was another burial of significance in this story, that of Gregorio N. Otero, the justice of the peace in Cubero who recorded Plácida's affidavit of her captivity, sent it to New Mexico territorial governor Lionel Sheldon, and subsequently had it published in the newspapers. Genealogical data collected by Arty Bibo in the 1960s

Grave of Plácida Romero to the left of Policarpio Romero (inside fence), at the Campo Santo Viejo de Cubero. Note the cross cut into the large rock at the head of her grave. Photograph by A. E. Roland.

indicates Gregorio Otero was also the father of Melquiades Otero, the man who transcribed the original "Corrido de Plácida Romero."

Plácida's child, Trinidad, who was adopted and raised by the Navajos, would have been about ninety-one or ninety-two years old in 1970. Her name among the Navajo people was Trinidad "Colorada" since she had red hair like her mother. During her marriage with a Navajo, they owned a fairly large herd of sheep.

Becoming the mother of a family, Trinidad Colorada lived the life of a Navajo, refused to return to her original family home in Cubero, and preferred to stay within the Navajo culture. She lived for many years at Baca in McKinley County near the Santa Fe railroad tracks about four miles west of Prewitt, New Mexico. She was finally discovered living there by a member of the extended family, and the information then found its way to Calletano and Plácida. Baca is still an active Navajo community with its own chapter house.

Amazingly, as Trinidad Colorada's half-sister, María Trinidad Romero, of Cubero, grew up, she became aware of her Navajo-raised sister and used to visit her at Baca. The two women were less than two years apart in age. Her family called

Plácida's brother, Calletano Romero, and his wife Apolonia (author's collection).

Trinidad Romero "La Apacha" because she was the offspring of Plácida's rape by an Apache during her mother's captivity. Plácida named this child Trinidad also in memory of her previous daughter, Trinidad (Colorada) Gallegos, since, by this time, Plácida had given up hope of finding her first Trinidad. In the year 1900, La Apacha married José Chávez, thus becoming Trinidad Romero Chávez.[9]

In the late 1960s, Trinidad Colorada was living in the area north of Borrego Pass in McKinley County, and Arty and I wanted to try to see her while she was still alive. We heard she spoke good Spanish, and all the older Navajos in the area seemed to know the story about her life. One of our major goals, maybe the most important, was to obtain the names, ages, and whereabouts of Trinidad Colorada's children. The rest of Plácida's descendants were well known, but here was a big gap. We also wanted to obtain her photograph. In the summer of 1970, we tried to locate Trinidad Colorada on the Navajo reservation. Through communications with Don and Fern Smouse, who owned and operated the Borrego Pass Trading Post for many years, we learned how to reach her property and heard that she would be glad to talk with us about her life story. On the day we had arranged to visit with her, during our trip from Albuquerque to the reservation, a severe summer storm with heavy hail boiled up, making the dirt roads on the reservation not only treacherous but totally impassable. We were extremely disappointed, but I had to turn the truck around and go back to Albuquerque; I couldn't jeopardize Arty's frail condition by getting the pickup stuck in the mud or sliding into a ditch in a remote area of the Navajo Nation.

I don't know who passed away first, Trinidad Colorada or Arty, but they both died in the early 1970s. Before we could schedule another trip, not in a rainy season, and working around Arty's health problems, both of their spirits had fluttered away, and so did our opportunity for continuing the documentation of Plácida's Navajo genealogical legacy.

7
Variations of the Plácida Story

As variants of Plácida's ballad developed in the intervening years, details of the story itself began to diverge from the version related in the original. Besides the ballad and newspapers, my other main sources of information were Arty's memory of the story he had heard while growing up in Cubero; interviews with family members and friends in Grants, Cubero, San Rafael, San Fidel, and Albuquerque in the 1960s; the affidavit given by Plácida to Gregorio N. Otero in Cubero on April 18, 1882; published army reports; genealogies; church records (marriage and birth certificates) from Cubero, San Fidel, Seboyeta, and San Rafael, New Mexico; and contemporary census records.

From version to version, there is considerable variation in the amount of time that Plácida was held captive by the Apaches in Mexico, with some stories claiming the Apaches kept her for three years.[1] Plácida stated in her affidavit the date of the attack was August 8, 1881, at Rancho Cebolla, and the apparent date of her escape described in the ballad was September 25, 1881, which pinpoints the timeline of her captivity. We know Plácida was back in Cubero the following April because the date of her deposition is April 18, 1882. Other evidence indicates that September 25 was indeed the day of her escape, so the duration of her captivity with Nana's band would have been forty-nine days. However, from her capture in early August 1881 until her return in early April 1882, she would have been absent for eight months from her home and children. It has been difficult for me to envision why it took so much time before Plácida was returned to Cubero. A wagon trip from Cubero to the area of El Paso would normally have been around fifteen days or less. It appears the time from when Plácida and Procopio arrived at the US–Mexico border after their escape to her arrival home was about six months. Assuming two months of communication time and another month of travel time, which still leaves around three months. The time of year would have been January, February, and March, the coldest part of the winter, and that could have postponed the return party's trip. Also, it is a reasonable assumption that Calletano waited until the state of New Mexico approved funds to pay the travel expenses for the return of Plácida and Procopio. That legislative act was passed on January 28, 1882, which would also account for the delay.

In some versions of the story, Apache war chief Mangus participated in the raiding party along with Apache leader Nana. Some versions of the ballad even mention Mangas Coloradas (Mangus's father), who was killed years earlier, in 1863. If Mangus was present, it is certain he would have been recognized by the federal Indian scouts, among who were many Chiricahuas, during one or more of the many battles between the federal troops and Nana's forces. Few people realize just how intimate the different Chiricahua tribes were, even though they disagreed and sometimes fought fiercely among themselves. There is no doubt the Indian scouts knew exactly who they were fighting, some of them even possibly being related to their enemies by marriage. No army reports mention Mangus during the long chase before Nana's group crossed the Mexican border. It is possible Mangus could have joined the raiders on their return or been at the San Joaquín rancheria when the renegades arrived.

Concerning Mangus, in one version of the story the Apaches kidnapped two children, the daughter Trinidad being eight or nine years old at the time, and the other an infant. This story says Trinidad was left with the Navajos while Plácida and the baby rode on with the Apaches. After a while, the baby became fretful and started to cry. At that time Mangus took the baby from Plácida and, holding it by the heels, swung it against a boulder, thus crushing its skull and tossed the corpse away. This version seems inaccurate for several reasons. First, had Trinidad been eight or nine years old, she surely would have looked for and recognized her mother when she returned from captivity and would have wanted to return to her. Second, although Plácida had a daughter about nine years of age, she was not involved in the story. Manuelita, an older sister of Trinidad, traveled with her uncle, Calletano, from the Cebolla Rancho to Cubero for the Fiesta de San Lorenzo the day before the murders. Finally, Plácida made no mention of the Indians kidnapping another child in her affidavit, which states: Trinidad was nine months old at the time. Some of their other children were staying with relatives in Cubero instead of with their parents during the actual raid.

Arising in later years was confusion over the role played in this story by Procopio García. Some versions indicate he was also kidnapped with Plácida from Rancho Cebolla. We do know Procopio was on the scene at Ysleta, Texas, near Juárez, Mexico, when Plácida was picked up by her brother and the other Cubero party members. The narrative of the ballad itself refers to him after Plácida escaped from her captivity. Our research established Procopio would have been nine years old at the time. Other sources have indicated he had been adopted by Domingo Gallegos and Plácida. This question is fully explained in the narrative portion of this story, and it turned out Procopio was actually a nephew of Domingo and had been abducted from Rancho García.

Another variation of Plácida's story indicates that when she was picked up by the Mexican civil authorities she was locked up in the jail at either Buenaventura or Galeana, Mexico, because she was believed to be a spy for the Apaches. As the story went, she was rescued from the jail by sympathetic townspeople who broke a hole in the jail roof one night and lowered a rope. From there she was taken in a one-horse buggy to the US border at Ysleta, Texas. This story came from Rosa Trujillo, but no mention of this occurrence is found in the newspaper account in *El Progresista* (El Paso del Norte) of Plácida's escape originating at Buenaventura, Mexico, and Plácida does not mention it in her affidavit.

Chief Victorio had a sister named Lozen who never married. She became a notable woman warrior, a superior horse thief, a revered diviner, and a renowned protector among the Warm Springs Apache people. She also outlived Victorio, not being present at the battle at Tres Castillos where he and most of the Warm Springs Chiricahuas were killed. The survivors related that due to Lozen's divining ability, they believed, had she been with Victorio at that time she would have warned them of the military presence and the whole band would have escaped from the Mexican troopers. Some authors have speculated Lozen was included in Nana's raiding party that kidnapped Plácida, although no author has presented a creditable citation for this detail.[2]

Again, no mention of Lozen is recorded from the federal Indian scouts, who certainly would have recognized her had she been present. Since Nana had left the party's women and children at the rancheria in San Joaquín Cañón, Lozen might have stayed with the women and children and been in charge of their protection. A primary consideration in Nana's mind would have been the protection of these few remaining remnants of the Warm Springs people that had survived the Mexican slaughter at Tres Castillos. Lozen would have been the best, and possibly only, choice for this duty. This is the most logical assumption that can be made in this case.[3]

A commonly asked question about Nana's raid is, How many warriors were with Nana? This is not an easy question to answer because the number varies considerably depending on what stage of the raid one is considering. Most historians agree that there were fifteen in Nana's party when they left Mexico. His stop early in the raid at the Mescalero Apache reservation netted him another twenty-five, bringing the count to forty. This count, minus attrition losses from battle (killed and wounded) continued until the war party crossed the Río Grande in central New Mexico going west where, military dispatches indicate, one-half of the Mescaleros left the group going south, down the river, and also doing mischief on the way back. This would have left approximately twenty-five. The next loss from Nana's band was at Mónica Springs, where two were wounded and the rest of the Mescaleros left. His force then would have been around thirteen. However, shortly thereafter Nana recruited some Navajos, probably from Alamo. Nobody knows for sure the count of the Navajos. Some historians have said ten, but there had to be more since twelve were reported at Rancho Cebolla. The combined group continued until the freighters and sheep ranchers were killed at Alamocita Creek. In this area Nana divided his group, and the next positive count we have is at the Rancho Cebolla massacre where seven Apaches, including Nana, and twelve Navajos were present and represented about half of the force, the other half raiding at Rancho García. Most of the Navajos quit Nana after these raids, so one can see the difficulty of ascertaining the total number of warriors. According to Plácida, after Nana returned to Mexico, only twelve warriors remained.

AFTERWORD

A Laguna Connection

Leslie Marmon Silko

PART I: INDIAN SLAVE TRADE IN THE SOUTHWEST

To better understand the circumstances of the abduction and captivity of Plácida Romero Gallegos in 1881, it is essential to review the history of the Indian slave trade in New Mexico prior to that time. Here I direct you to L. R. Bailey's excellent scholarly work, *Indian Slave Trade in the Southwest*, first published in 1966. The extensive research into the baptismal records of the Catholic Church and other public records that Bailey relied upon were conducted by two eminent ethnohistorians, David M. Brugge and J. Lee Carroll.

According to Bailey, even before the Great Pueblo Revolt of 1680, the Spanish authorities determined that slave raids would be used to punish unfriendly Indian tribes. The Spaniards quickly learned that although the Indians were fearless of death, the thought of their children being kidnapped and sold into slavery terrified them. So the Spaniards recruited Indian allies to make slave raids against Indians hostile to the Spaniards. This was Spain's usual policy: to pit one group against another. It guaranteed that the tribes would remain at odds with one another and could not again unite against the Spaniards as they had in 1680.[1]

Poor tribes became powerful with the guns they got in trade for the Indian captives they took. The tribes that suffered the attacks of the slave hunters lost everything, and hid in remote mountains.[2] Rendezvous camps sprang up near Spanish settlements along the Pecos, Río Grande, San Pedro, and Santa Cruz Rivers, where traders met with Indians to exchange human captives for gunpowder, steel, and whiskey. At Tucson, Chihuahua, El Paso, Albuquerque, Bernalillo, Santa Fe, Abiquiu, Taos, Pecos, Cebolleta, and Cubero, drunken depraved exhibitions at slave markets featured the rapes of captive Indian girls by slave dealers.[3]

Between 1700 and 1760 the names of eight hundred Apaches were recorded in baptismal and other Catholic Church records in New Mexico parishes.[4] Forced baptisms were performed on the captive children, who often were given to the volunteers who went along with the Spanish troops on military assaults against the Apaches and the Navajos. The Indian captives were seldom part of the Spanish families. Church records refer to them as "servants," but their status remained always that of slaves.

The Spanish governors of New Mexico not only permitted the Indian slave trade, they participated in and profited from it. More money could be made from one slave-hunting expedition of three or four weeks than could be made in a year of subsistence farming or ranching in New Mexico. Lucrative for a few but costly for the wider community, the chaos and hatred sparked by Indian slavery resulted in intertribal violence that kept away settlers and investment, preventing the rich commerce that Spaniards dreamed of.[5] Tragically it was usually the ordinary people, subsistence farmers and ranchers like Plácida Romero and her husband, who suffered the wrath of the Apaches, not the affluent families that bought and sold Indian slaves.

Nothing changed when New Mexico won independence from Spain. The Mexican authorities in New Mexico also trafficked in Indian slaves. Upon their takeover of the New Mexico Territory in 1846, General Kearny and the US authorities saw the violence and chaos resulting from the slave trade and realized at once that New Mexico Territory would be ungovernable until the Indian slave trade stopped and all captives, Indian and Mexican alike, were returned to their people.[6] However, the wealthy, powerful Mexican and white families of New Mexico stubbornly resisted all efforts by the US authorities to free their Indian "servants." A number of US authorities themselves had Indian "servants."[7]

On a number of occasions the Navajo leaders complained to the US authorities that even though they had complied in good faith and had given up all their captives, the Mexicans and whites had not. Whenever possible, the Navajos always sought the return of their captive children by filing lawsuits in the territorial courts.[8] The fact was, from 1846, when the US authorities began to govern the New Mexico Territory until 1881, the year of Plácida's kidnapping, the Indian slave trade continued much as it had for two hundred years before the United States seized the territory from Mexico. Because of the failure of the US government to stop the Indian slave trade, tragedy befell Plácida Romero and her family in early August of 1881.

Apache warriors driven half-crazy by rage and despair at the destruction of their people went on a rampage in New Mexico in the summer of 1881. Her husband murdered, Plácida and her infant daughter, Trinidad, were abducted from their small ranch in Cebolla Canyon southwest of Cubero. Cubero was the site of an early and important Spanish fort, and from the 1700s, the town was a major slave-trading center. Perhaps the Apache warriors came to the Cubero area to take captives in retaliation for all the Apache children sold at Cubero's slave markets.

A few months before I read the manuscript of *The Ballad of Plácida Romero*, I traveled to Ciudad Chihuahua for the first time. There I was fortunate to meet and spend time with the descendants of the Apaches who lived in the mountains of Chihuahua. The people I met were so generous and warm, so welcoming I fell in love with them and the beautiful mountains of their old stronghold. So when I read the details of Plácida's escape in the manuscript, I was greatly impressed but not surprised at the enormous compassion and kindness of the women who freed Plácida.

Truly the heroes of the ballad of Plácida Romero are these Apache women who felt sorry for Plácida and took the risk of helping her escape the cruelty of the warriors. At a time when bounties were paid for Apache scalps, the Apache women gave Plácida clothing, food, and a burro to ride to safety. But not surprisingly, the ballad makes no mention of the compassion of the Apache women; predictably, the ballad praises the God and Saints of the Catholic Church.

Once she was home, Plácida Romero's ordeal was not over. When she sought the return of her baby daughter from the Navajos, a corrupt federal Indian agent at Fort Defiance dealt Plácida a terrible blow. The Indian agent, Galen Eastman, was stealing Navajo rations and selling them. He bought the silence of the Navajos by refusing to force them to give back Plácida's baby girl, Trinidad Colorada. Not impassioned letters to the newspapers nor fiery editorials nor even the territorial governor could trump the Indian agent's federal jurisdiction, so Trinidad Colorada remained with her adoptive Navajo parents.

Despite all that happened, when they were adults, Trinidad la Apacha, who was born to Plácida after her abduction and rape, visited her sister, Trinidad Colorada, who married a Navajo and lived southwest of San Mateo Mountain (Mt. Taylor today). In the end the sisters were united.

PART 2: THE LAGUNAS, THE APACHES AND THE NAVAJOS

As I read the manuscript of *The Ballad of Plácida Romero*, I realized that long ago my great grandma A'mooh told me about the rampaging band of warriors in the summer of 1881. Her uncle and two cousins were herding sheep southeast of Laguna behind the big black mesa near Swanee in the El Rito valley. A'mooh said the Apaches used the mesa to shield themselves from view as they approached, and crept up behind the shepherds to kill them.

After the Apache attacks, the Laguna Regulars, with my great grandfather, Robert G. Marmon, and his older brother, Walter G. Marmon, pursued the Apaches who were part of the same group that kidnapped Plácida Romero. The Apaches outsmarted Grandpa Marmon and the Laguna Regulars; instead of going west and north as some predicted, the Apaches headed straight south for their stronghold in the mountains of Chihuahua. Around this time came reports that some Apache snipers stalked the Marmon brothers and the Laguna Regulars for a chance to shoot the white men, but never got the chance.

Grandma A'mooh's accounts of the Laguna "scouts," as she called them, made a powerful impression on me. I wrote the short story "A Geronimo Story" about the Laguna Regulars chasing Geronimo, and how, maybe, the Laguna Regulars knew better than to catch up with the rampaging Apaches. I was always relieved that my great grandpa Marmon and his brother never killed anyone; the Marmons in Ohio were Quakers.

The event Grandma A'mooh was proudest to relate was the time nobody was harmed but some Navajos ran off a herd of Laguna sheep. A group of Laguna men (not the Regulars) decided to go after the stolen sheep. When the Lagunas caught up with them (because sheep don't travel very fast), it turned out to be an old Navajo man and two boys who took the sheep. The Lagunas asked, "Why did you steal our sheep?" And the old Navajo man said, "Because we are starving to death." So the Lagunas gave them four sheep and told them "The next time you are starving just come ask us and we'll give you sheep, you don't need to steal them."

The Laguna Regulars existed long before my great grandfather and his brother came to Laguna. In the time of Spanish rule, the pueblos were required to defend their boundaries from encroachments by the Apaches and Navajos. According to Catholic Church baptismal records, from 1774 to 1780, thirteen young Navajo children were baptized at Laguna.[9] Now I wonder, did the Laguna Regulars in the 1770s get paid off with young captives? The Pueblos, like the Navajos, adopted the captives into their families, where they were treated like family members and married into the tribe.

PART 3: JUANA

Long before I knew anything about the Indian slave trade in New Mexico, I'd heard Grandma Lillie's stories about Juana, the Navajo captive who lived with them and cared for them when they were children.

On Memorial Day when I was twelve or thirteen, Grandma Lillie asked me if I wanted to go with her to take flowers to old Juana's grave. Juana died around 1920 when she was more than one hundred years old. We filled jars and cans with water and then we cut some roses and lilacs from Grandma A'mooh's yard. Grandma Lillie drove us to the south side of Laguna village, and then down a dirt road near the old bridge across the river. Juana's grave was in an old graveyard no longer in use. A low wall of dark lava rock surrounded the pale gray river sand; in the corners of the walls, dry weeds, scraps of paper and debris piled in drifts. Not many people visited the graveyard anymore. The graves had no carved gravestones but were marked with flat pieces of sandstone or black lava rock. I saw the remains of a few wooden crosses. That day it took Grandma Lillie awhile to find the stones that marked Juana's grave. She hadn't been there for years but that year, for some reason, she decided to take Juana flowers.

Grandma cleared away the tumbleweeds tangled with bits of paper and dried remains of flowers, and I picked up the scattered cans and jars that once served as vases. Juana's grave was marked with a small pile of fist-sized black lava stones. Grandma Lillie said Juana was captured by Mexican slave catchers when she was just a little girl. Years later Lincoln freed the slaves, but by then thirty years had passed and Juana no longer spoke the Navajo language, and worse, she did not know from where she had been stolen.

I had the impression from Grandma Lillie that Juana came to work for their family at the time of the Emancipation Proclamation. Recently I learned there is much more to Juana's story than Grandma Lillie told me.

Grandma Lillie said Juana was the one who really mothered her and her eleven brothers and sisters, not my great Grandma Helen. Grandma Helen followed the practice of the wealthy Mexican and white women at the time, which meant she took to her bed as soon as she was pregnant, and did not leave her bed again until two months after the birth. It was Juana who cared for the children while their mother awaited the next birth. Juana bathed them and fed them, Juana rocked them and held them when they were scared or sick, not their mother. Juana was well into her eighties when Grandma Lillie was born.

I remember Great Grandma Helen vividly in her black dress and black sweater, rolling her own little cigarettes from a small sack of Bull Durham tobacco. When she came to visit, she discussed family gossip in Spanish so us kids couldn't understand. I can't remember her hugging us; she hardly seemed to notice us.

Grandma Helen was born to Josephine Romero, whose mother was a Luna, one of the founding families of Los Lunas. Josephine Romero married a Whittington, the son of an English merchant and his wife who was a daughter of the Chávez family, also founders of Los Lunas.

When Grandma Lillie was a girl she called her grandmother, Josephine Romero Whittington, "Grandma Whip." Grandma Whip wore a black braided leather belt that she could quickly remove to use as a whip. My father remembered Grandma Whip too. He said the children called her "Grandma Whip" because whenever they visited her, the first thing she did was warn them not to touch anything in her house by saying "Grandma whip! Grandma whip if you touch!"

The terrible whippings which were part of child rearing in Grandma Lillie's family, and which affected my father and terrorized my sisters and me, were a legacy from Grandma Whip. But it wasn't until I learned more about Juana's story that I realized where the abuse originated, and the tragedy long ago that resulted from those whippings.

Years ago I read L. C. Bailey's book on Indian slavery; but this time, as I reread the book to prepare to write this essay, certain details stood out: a young Navajo woman released from her captivity in 1852, complained to the US military officer who freed her that the Mexican family stripped her naked and whipped her often.[10] Here it was, an account very much like the terrible whippings that were part of Juana's story, the part of the story Grandma Lillie was ashamed to tell: how Juana came into Grandma Whip's family.

In 1823, Spanish governor José Antonio Vizcara launched an assault against the Navajos. During this military campaign, four young Navajo girls, sisters, the youngest only three years old, were captured and brought to Los Lunas, to the house of Grandma Whip's brother. Did he buy the little Navajo girls from a slave trader, or were they the loot he got for volunteering to accompany the Spanish troops on the assault? Did someone owe him a gambling debt and give him the little girls in payment or were they a bribe to curry his favor?

If Grandma Whip was quick to take off the leather belt to whip her small grandchildren, then her brother must have been the Devil himself with the young Navajo girls. He must not have given the girls any rest. He must have whipped them so brutally their lives became intolerable, because finally, the three older girls had to act. They killed their torturer with poison. With the son of two prominent families dead at the hands of Indian servants, the local authorities had to act at once so the other Indian servants didn't get any ideas. Three young Navajo girls were hanged at once, and only the youngest girl, too young to have participated in the crime, was spared. This was Juana.

Did the wealthy families of Los Lunas send their Indian "servants" to watch the hangings as a precaution? Did they make little Juana watch her sisters die? Did Juana understand then that her last link with her family and her people died with her sisters, and there would be no reunion for her?

Poor little Juana became the inheritance, the property of Grandma Whip, the dead man's sister. Juana found herself among strange people where mothers left their babies to the servants for care. How different Juana's family was—her mother and aunts and grandmothers and father and grandfathers and older sisters—how much they must have loved her until that terrible moment when she was seized by the kidnappers. It was this love that must have sustained her, and kept her from dying of sadness; it was this love her family gave her that Juana gave to my grandmother and others as they were born. Juana gave them love in a house where there was little love for children. It was Juana who intervened for the next generation of children, so they might know mother love and one day love their babies as their own mother had not.

Grandma Lillie and I took flowers to Juana's grave, but we never visited Grandma Helen's grave in Albuquerque. I know how to locate Juana's grave in the old graveyard at Laguna but I have no idea where to find Grandma Helen's grave.

PART 4: TWO SISTERS CALLED TRINIDAD

Plácida must have been an extraordinary woman, not just because she survived the weeks with the murderous warriors on the run, but because she was able to appeal to the Apache women who aided her, and because of how she lived her life after she returned to Cubero. She kept her vow to make a religious play out of her kidnapping and escape. Perhaps because of the religious interpretation she gave to her ordeal, the rape and the subsequent birth of her daughter, Trinidad la Apacha, were not obstacles to Plácida's remarriage. God sent the ordeal as a test of faith—not just Plácida's faith, but the faith of the entire community. Even her failure to get back her daughter adopted by the Navajos could be viewed as part of God's plan.

It must have been too painful for Plácida to visit her stolen daughter even years later. But when they were adults, Trinidad la Apacha went to visit her sister, Trinidad Colorada at Baca, New Mexico, west of Grants. This relationship between the two sisters as adults interests me very much. I understand why Trinidad went to see her half-sister. Curiosity. Her mother, Plácida, must have talked about the way the Navajos lived. But it must have been more; it was she whose father was an Apache warrior who lived in the wild mountains of Chihuahua. Trinidad would have only to glance into a mirror to be reminded she did not look like others in the family. Her story was known and told by everyone in the community; the hand of God brought her there. Sometimes she must have felt lonely, being so different from others in Cubero; it was then she must have thought about her sister adopted by the Navajos; her sister, Trinidad Colorada, didn't look like the other children either, and there was a story about her too: about the way the Apaches gave her to the Navajos because a baby could not survive the trek back to Chihuahua. One of the raiders who gave the baby to the Navajos might have been Plácida's rapist, Trinidad la Apacha's father.

I do not know the number of visits the two sisters had over the years. I hope it was a large number. I remember Cubero when I was growing up; Navajos were not welcome there, so Trinidad la Apacha had to go to the Navajo encampment to see her sister. I hope they found some comfort with one another on those visits.

In the end the captives were the ones blessed with grace; the captives had the riches of spirit and humanity; the merchant slave-keepers, fast on the whip, were corrupted beyond redemption; devils came for them and carried them out the door straight to Hell before they died. I should know—they were my ancestors.

Plácida's story, Juana's story—murder, kidnapping, rape, and slavery—they are familiar stories in any country torn by war. The New Mexico Territory was at war for more than three hundred years as the indigenous people fought to resist the invasion by the slave hunters and other agents of the Church and the Crown.

The story of the two sisters, Plácida's story, and Juana's story exemplify the tragedy of those horrendous centuries of the slave trade in the New Mexico Territory. Even now, the ghosts drift around the slave market towns of Tucson and El Paso, Abiquiu and Taos. What do they want? They outnumber the living ten to one. On hot summer afternoons in the bosque along the river, one can still hear the leaves on the cottonwood tree rustle the way they did each time another of Juana's sisters was hanged.

ACKNOWLEDGMENTS

One of the major helpers along the trail of getting this story together was Mr. Robert E. "Bob" Forrester Jr. He was a chemist who worked in the aerospace industry in Fort Worth, Texas for many years and was also a very perceptive amateur archaeologist. Bob excavated many prehistoric Indian ruin sites for Arty on his Los Pilares Ranch. He wrote comprehensive reports on each dig site and submitted copies to the Laboratory of Anthropology in Santa Fe as well as to Arty. Bob was the person who had the tape recorder when Arty was ready to record the basics of this story at his ranch home at Los Pilares in the evening of June 10, 1970. Bob Forrester died in 1996 and his ashes and those of his wife Billie Jean were scattered on the former Bibo ranch.

For help with the corrido translation, I was introduced to and became close friends with Paul Dooley and his family. Paul was a teacher at Grants High School and was also a degreed Spanish linguist. Paul and his wife Connie had spent many years in Spain. About 1975, Paul and I were able, with the aid of some powerful magnification, to decipher the illegible text in the original ballad and complete the translation. I remember spending many evenings at the Dooleys' house in the Zuni Mountains going over the ballad to make sure the translation was acceptable and enjoying Connie's unbelievably delectable paella. Paul passed away in August of 2003 at his home in Tampa, Florida. Recently, Enrique R. Lamadrid, professor emeritus and distinguished professor of Spanish in the Department of Spanish and Portuguese at the University of New Mexico, helped me to enhance the translation.

For field research of the Apache routes through the Dátil Mountains and northward, I am indebted to several people who live and/or ranch in these areas. The land is home predominantly to large ranches, the Quién Sabe, Criswell, York, Mertz/Major, Bar 15, and the Red Lake operations. Guidance and location of old Indian trails and early routes of travel through this country came from six primary sources: Norman Cleaveland (deceased) for the Dátil Mountain country; Mike McWhorter (deceased), born in the area and long-time manager of the Quién Sabe Ranch; Gene Baca and Tucker McHugh, residents on the Criswell Ranch; Jim Lesley, manager of the York Ranch; and Buddy Major (deceased), raised in the area and former owner of the Mertz/Major Ranch. Guidance in the Bar 15 country (the former brand of the previous ranch owner, Carl Wilson, and present ranch name now belonging to the Acoma Land and Cattle Co. in the area east of the Blue Water Vega) was provided by David Marmon. David is a second cousin of Lee Marmon and the son of Fred Marmon, a land surveyor who surveyed much of that country for many decades.

Several of the photographs in this book are by gifted Laguna artist Lee Marmon (1925–2021). At age twenty-one, Marmon returned home from the Aleutian Islands and World War II to work in his father's trading post at Laguna Pueblo. In time, Marmon went west to California where he became the official photographer for the Bob Hope Desert Classic Golf Tournament. Working in Hollywood at the same time he also captured images of some of the film industry's leading celebrities, including Frank Sinatra, Sammy Davis Jr., Dean Martin, and Raquel Welch. Yet Marmon never lost sight of his spiritual roots and he returned to Laguna every year to live and work with friends and tribal leaders. His photo murals today grace the Denver International Airport, the Peabody Museum of Archaeology in Cambridge, Massachusetts, the Indian Pueblo Cultural Center in Albuquerque, the Alkek Library at Texas State University in San Marcos, Phillips Academy at Andover, Massachusetts, and the University of California Davis. In 2008, the University of New Mexico's Center for Southwest Research purchased his valuable negative collection.

The Marmon and Bibo families were contemporaries in the early development of the New Mexico Territory. They were merchant families, operating mercantiles and trading posts mostly in central and western New Mexico. The Marmons intermarried with the Laguna Pueblo people and one of the Bibos married into Acoma Pueblo. These families knew and did business with one another for many years, and it was through Arty that I met Lee Marmon in the early 1960s. Through the years I have spent many good times with Lee on photo shoots, at his family ranch, Dripping Springs, and at his home in Laguna and I remember fondly his daughters, Leslie (Leslie Marmon Silko), Wendy, and Gigi, as well as his wife and son, Kathy and Leland Jr. Recently I have become acquainted with Lee's other son, Chris, and his wife Michele. Arty and I had discussed, while he was still living, the picture possibilities that would enhance this story. Finally, in 2005 or 2006, Lee and I scheduled the field trips to capture the photographs of the story locations I had previously located. Lee Marmon succumbed to old age at ninety-five years on March 31, 2021. Another good longtime friend and photographer, Kelly Gatlin, from Dátil, New Mexico, doing business as La Luz Photo (laluzphoto.com), also graciously contributed some of his photos.

Leslie Marmon Silko, novelist, poet, and short-story writer, upon reading this manuscript, became immediately intrigued with the memories, related by her grandmothers, of the involvements that her family, the Marmons, had with this tragic occurrence. She very rapidly pinpointed incidents and recollections of family stories that are intimately connected with this historical event and readily agreed to write an essay for this work. Few in the Southwest today understand the relations between the different cultures and between human beings as deeply as Silko. Although educated at the University of New Mexico in English and law, she was also educated by grandmothers and aunts in the traditional stories of the Laguna people. Silko has written a book of poems, *Laguna Woman*, and an anthology of Native American stories in *The Man to Send Rain Clouds: Contemporary Stories by American Indians*. Her novels, *Ceremony* and *Almanac of the Dead* as well as a collection of essays, *Yellow Woman and a Beauty of the Spirit: Essays on Native American Life Today* have attracted much critical acclaim. Silko has won prizes, fellowships, and grants from organizations such as the National Endowment for the Arts and the Boston Globe. Today, Silko lives and writes in Tucson, Arizona, with a menagerie of pets including parrots, macaws, and rattlesnakes.

In 2001, I became acquainted with, and a good friend of, Jerry D. Thompson, Regents Professor of History at Texas A&M International University in Laredo, Texas. My wife and I lived across the street and had become good friends with Jerry's father (now deceased) in Quemado, New Mexico. Dr. Thompson is among the best and most prolific historians of the Civil War in the Southwest. With dozens of books and articles to his credit, he is a leading authority of the history of the United States–Mexico borderlands. A past president of the Texas State Historical Association, he holds a doctorate from Carnegie Mellon University and has received numerous awards from the Texas Historical Commission, Western Writers of America, Texas State Historical Association, Historical Society of New Mexico, and the Arizona Historical Society. Jerry graciously and with much interest extended his help in draft readings and organization of the manuscript as well as providing and pointing me toward sources of historical archives I would not have found on my own. He and I enjoyed many field trips undertaken to track down some of the more obscure historical connections.

Chair of the Department of Spanish and Portuguese at the University of New Mexico before retiring, Enrique R. Lamadrid is a leading scholar of Hispanic folklore, folk music, ethnopoetics, Chicano literature, and Latin American poetry, as well as the cultures of Mexico, the Caribbean, and the indigenous peoples of the Andes. For six years, Lamadrid also directed the Chicano Hispano Mexicano Studies program at the University of New Mexico. He is a Fulbright scholar, Rockefeller fellow, and recipient of several awards from the University of New Mexico and the University of Chicago. Dr. Lamadrid has published numerous books, monographs, essays, and articles.

In the spring of 2006, at an historical symposium in Socorro, New Mexico, I was fortunate to be introduced to Dr. Lamadrid. During our conversation I became aware that he had also done considerable research into this piece of New

Mexico history/folklore, along with his good friends and professional colleagues, photographer Miguel Gandert and student Herman Bustamante. Arty Bibo and I had done our primary research with family members on Plácida's side in the 1960s. With Herman and his family, Enrique worked on this project in the mid 1980s. Arty and I obtained considerable material from Anna Mae Starr, a descendant of Calletano Romero (Plácida's brother). Enrique's research centered on interviews with Feliz Bustamante, Rosa Trujillo, and Veronica Rickart, who all still sing Plácida's ballad. After Anna Mae's death, ethnomusicologist Brenda Romero introduced Enrique to Mary Daley Bledsoe, Anna Mae's younger sister, who taught their family version to Brenda, who still sings it. Enrique's involvement provided indispensable material in this historical discourse as he is a noted authority on New Mexico corridos/inditas and folklore. During the research that Arty and I conducted in the 1960s, we could not find the music that accompanied this ballad. We came to believe the music was never written down or recorded. Thanks to the work of Dr. Lamadrid, the music of several of ten versions of this ballad have also been recovered and preserved.

I am indebted to Mary Stella Bledsoe and William Bledsoe of Fort Collins, Colorado, for my learning of the existence of the letter published in *El Progesista* on October 14, 1881. Mary and Will have also done a great deal of research into this story from the point of view of Calletano's branch of the family, since Mary is a descendant of Calletano. (Calletano is properly spelled in Spanish with a "Y" as well. I use the double "L" because that is the spelling used in the ballad.) Mary passed away in January 2010 and I grieve that she did not get to see this manuscript. I am also thankful to them for providing the genealogy of Plácida's descendants.

Of course, Arty's many interviews with Rosa Trujillo in the 1960s and her gracious gifts of Plácida's and Domingo's personal items and the original transcription of the corrido were invaluable and beyond comparison. Rosa was a daughter of Manuelita Armijo and granddaughter of Plácida.

Carol A. Macauly-Jameson, a lecturer in anthropology among other things at Baylor University, and her husband Bryan, have been friends of the author for many years. I am extremely lucky to have their prodigious talents represented here with the great archaeological work at the Armijo homestead and exceptional GIS maps of the homestead and of Rancho Cebolla.

One of the most knowledgeable authors on the Apaches Victorio and Nana and their wars is Dr. Robert N. "Bob" Watt. He is a lecturer in the Department of Political Science and International Studies (POLSIS) at the University of Birmingham, United Kingdom. His main research concerns the Apache years, 1860–86, with special emphasis on 1879–81. In 2012, I hosted Dr. Watt and toured him to some of the locations of Nana's fights that I had become aware of through my research into Plácida's kidnapping travails and travels. His three-volume series concentrating on the Victorio and Nana era battles is by far the most comprehensive work to date on these subjects. Through back-and-forth communications, Watt and I have considered most of the discernible possibilities of military movements after the abduction of Plácida. While my focus has been on Plácida's captivity by Nana and Watt's has been on the military; our combined paths have provided a good logical trail and I am considerably thankful for his excellent work.

Thanks are due to Durwood Ball, Cindy Tyson, Meg Frisbee, Donna Peterson, peer reviewers, and the staff of the *New Mexico Historical Review* for their patience and undeniably needed editorial assistance in publishing an early draft of this work in the summer 2011 issue. This version is greatly expanded, with changes in the writing style to a less academic format, and significant additions of photographs, maps, and historical connections subsequently discovered and confirmed. This new edition also includes a photocopy of the original transcription of the ballad that manifestly belongs in the public domain.

I am also deeply indebted to the very talented staff of the Museum of New Mexico Press, especially Lisa Pacheco. She, like a good shepherd, kept this lone maverick on the right trail and pointed in the right direction. Her very capable management of this book project is invaluable. Also, Beth Hadas, former director of UNM Press, did a wonderful job on the copyediting.

A world of thanks must go to my wife Nelcine, mostly for her years of patience.

APPENDIX 1
Original Spanish Corrido Transcription
As presented to Arthur Bibo by Rosa Trujillo

The following nine pages contain a photocopy of the original transcription of the Corrido de Plácida Romero. It is reproduced here since it is a document in the neighborhood of 135 years old, at this writing, and, I suspect, there will be considerable interest by many scholars, historians, and descendants of Plácida in studying its contents. Being so old and extremely fragile, the original cannot survive much handling and inspection and should remain in archival conditions as much as possible. The permanent home for this document will be the archives of the Museum of New Mexico in Santa Fe.

The order of these pages here is as they appear in the original document, although they do not present the story in the correct chronological sequence.

En el dia de San Lorenso
Serea de las seis del dia
asi seria yo pienso
cuando esto nos susedia
que vi ami Esposo muriendo
como pues lo resistiria
   A Dios lla.
Ay Esposo desgraciado
a Dios fino Compañero
quisa no tenias Cuñado
ni parientes en Cubero
puesto quedastes tirado
adentro de un gallinero
   A Dios lla.
Este mundo escandaloso
no es mas q. un aparato
Sevolla Rancho famoso
por que fuistes tan Ingrato
donde Matan ami Esposo
Ya mi q. me lleva el tato
   ¡a Dios lla.!

Madre mia dolorosa
Padre mio San José
la, pues madre amorosa
te lo pido por mersed
Cuida a mis hijas piadosa
pues huerfanas hoy se ven.
    A Dios lla me boy.
Madrecita de la Lus
Madre de mi Corason
Pidele a tu hijo Jesus
me saque de esta prision
pues q. sucumbio en la Crus
tenga de mi Compacion.
    A. Dios lla,,
Boy sintiendo un gran dolor
por q. dejé a mis hijitas
Manuelita la Mayor
cuida de tus ermanitas
pues lla les falto el Calor
quedaron huerfanitas
    A. Dios lla,,

A mi Padre y a mi Ermano
les encargo a mis hijitas
no te olvides Calletano
de tus Caras Sobrinitas
hay se quedan huerfanitas
en este Mundo tirano.
    A Dios Pa.

Adios Padres desgraciados
hechenme Su Vendicion
y esten siempre Consevidado
en Cualesquiera Ocacion
Con estos Yndios malvado
esta Varbara nacion
    A Dios Pa.

Adios Madresita mia
A Dios mi querido Padre
Jusgen como quedaria
Con este Crecido afare.
Viendo aji mi Compañia
rerolcandose en su Sangre
    A Dios Pa.

A Dios. Madresita mia
duelase de mi desgracia
ha Dios todos mis Vesinos
A Dios mi ogar y mi Casa
A Dios tambien a mis parientes
A Dios Madre Mª Cacia.
  A. Dios Pª. 4
Desde el dia que salí
del parage mas sercano
Con mucho Cuidado fui
Cuando en cumbrera el gn Van
Ver si Via benir
a mi padre ho, a mi Ermano.
  A. Dios Pª.
En la mesa de la Escoba
Zequedo mi hija querida
Hay Sierra de la Cebolla
porque fuistes tan Esquiba
las piedras los palos lloran
a verme Salir Cautiba.
  A. Dios Pª.

Llegue al Ojito Salado
Con aquel dolor ardiente
Como es paraje mentado
Alli esperaba la gente
A Dios Ombero afamado
sete acabo lo Caliente.
  A. Dios Ma.
En las minas que el acaso
pegue un suspiro Velos
y como llegue despacio
hay bi que mataron dos
el hijo llamado Ygnacio
y su padre Juan de Dios.
  A. Dios Pa,
El dia y Ma llegue
Serea de San Buenabentura
a Dios le pedi mersed
Como una Anjelis Criatura
y al patriarca San José
tambien a la Virgen pura

Ho Dios Ya me siento libre
por tu Gran poder
Ya mis padres ya mis hijas
espero volver aver.
Veite sinco de Setiembre
Ya Dios se compadecio
Ya le pedi humildem.te
Y mis suplicas hoyó
ayi nos sintio la jente
y al momento nos sigio.
    O Dios Ya,, me siento libre
Luego que reconocio
Ser jente la que venia
que salieramos de alli
parese llegado el dia
no te retires de mi
dije ha Procopio Garcia
    Oh. Dios Ya,,

Si la Corte Selestial
eselame a San Agustin
propusieron terminar
de mi cautiberio el fin
me propongo no olvidar
el Canon de San Juaquin.
Oh Dios lla.
En que trabajos me he visto
con estos indios tiranos
ho Sierra madre del Cristo
donde Dios me dio sus manos
y donde libre me he visto
y en las manos de Cristianos
Ilo. Dios lla.
Ya yo quisas me olvide
Ya no se acuerdan de mi
llo luego los no tirie
desde el dia que Sali
lla me toca padeser
Con este Signo naci
Ilo Dios lla,

A Dios le pido memoria
y permiso al mundo entero
para dictar esta historia
de la Jolanda Romero
que tal ves sera notoria
en y fuera de Cubero y padres
A Dios ya me boy sin duda
a mis padres y a mis hijas
Cuando las Volvere aver.
Año de mil ochocientos
Ochenta y uno llovioso
el dia de San Lorenso
quiso el todo Poderoso
que me quedara Sintiendo
a mi hijita y a mi Esposo
 A Dios Va

Sentandonos a almorsar
Senos llego la Ocasion
quien lo avia de pensar
que esta barbara nacion
nos quisieran Cautibar
y pegarnos a Traision
 i a Dios Va

Hay esposo de mi Vida
y Men que dolor murio
Con una mortal herida
que aun ni sus harmas uso
Biendose Salir Cautiba
a Dios el Alma entregó.
    A. Dios Ma
Tan fuerte Golpe le an dado
que con el fierro de herrar
Vi sus sesos derramados
Sin poderlo remediar
hay Domingo desgraciado
Como no te he de llorar.
    A. D. Ma
San Lorenso milagroso
por que escojistes tu dia
mostrandote reguroso
quisas Ma me Convenia
que mataran a mi esposo
tambien a Jose M.
    A. Dios Ma,

APPENDIX 2
Arthur G. Bibo 1899–1972

John L. Kessell

> "Stop just beyond the next cattle guard. See that long, low mesa on the right a couple of miles away? See where it drops off? There's a kind of cone-shaped little peak in the distance. The Acomas call that . . . ."
> [—Arty Bibo]

Arthur Bibo had been blind for three years when he began showing me around his *patria chica,* that area of New Mexico he knew so well—from the valley of the Rio Puerco west to the Continental Divide, from Mount Taylor south beyond Acoma pueblo twenty-five or thirty miles—the province Fray Marcos de Niza called the Kingdom of Acus. Only a man of remarkable perception who had walked and ridden and trailed cattle over it for forty years could have recalled so vividly without sight every feature of that vast, broken landscape. Being one with the land gave him a strength that neither deafness nor blindness could overcome.

Born in Bernalillo, January 4, 1899, raised in the little Hispanic community of Cubero where his father Emil and his uncles operated the Bibo Brothers store and trading post, Artie [sic] Bibo grew up with three cultures. When he was twelve the family moved to San Francisco, California, for the children's schooling. He came home to New Mexico in 1917. Already the partial loss of his hearing had forced him to give up a formal higher education at Stanford University or an artist's career. He would be a rancher instead.

He became much more, a rancher-ecologist. He observed and learned the unique lay of the land, the plants and grasses, the insects, the archaeological sites the weather, and the people, the sheepherders, government agents, and archaeologists. And he found ways to share his knowledge. He worked to found the Lava Soil and [Water] Conservation District; he corrected maps for the USGS; he urged the public acquisition and protection of the lava beds; he invited universities to excavate the rich prehistoric sites on his Los Pilares Ranch.

After Congress passed the Indian Claims Act of 1946, Artie [sic] Bibo's neighbors, the Acoma Indians, asked for his help in preparing their claim. Wholeheartedly he devoted himself to the task. With the few old men of the pueblo who still remembered, he went out and mapped the Acomas' traditional boundaries. He corroborated his field notes with painstaking documentary research. Although he was dropped from the case after two years in favor of a team of PhDs, his work remained basic to the settlement achieved in 1971.

As he chased strays and studied petroglyphs, Arthur Bibo conceived an idea that became a vision with him, a cultural center and field school where scholars of a dozen disciplines and interested persons from all over could come to study, appreciate, and help protect this unique region of New Mexico. . . .

When he died, on December 13, 1972, this warm, undespairing rancher, ecologist, and humanitarian was at work on a composite map of the Kingdom of Acus showing geographic features, historic place names, boundaries, surveys, and the vestiges of prehistoric cultures. Arthur Bibo had lost his sight but not his vision.

The eulogy above is reprinted from New Mexico Historical Review *48, no. 2 (April 1973): 165–66.*

APPENDIX 3
Descendants of María Plácida Romero

María Plácida ROMERO (b.11 May 1853; d.1902? – Cubero, Valencia, NM Territory)

sp: Domingo GALLEGOS (b.6 May 1845-NM Terty; m.7 Jan 1868; d.8 Aug 1881-La Cebolla, Valencia, NM Terty)

    Felipa GALLEGOS (b.1865-NM Terty)

    sp: Jose Antonio CHAVES (m.24 Sep 1883)

        Teofila CHAVES (b.7 Apr 1885)

    Manuela GALLEGOS (b.16 Dec 1868-NM Terty; d.1948)

    sp: Antonio ARMIJO (m.24 Sep 1883)

        Domingo ARMIJO (b.22 Sep 1884)

        Margarita ARMIJO (b.10 Jun 1886-Cubero, NM Terty)

        sp: Fabian VALLEJOS (m.9 Jul 1901)

            Feliz VALLEJOS (b.Abt 1900)

            sp: Quilimaco DIAZ (b.Abt 1894; m.19 Oct 1915)

        Veneranda ARMIJO (b.8 Dec 1889-Cubero, NM Terty)

        Rosenda (Rosa) ARMIJO (b.1 Dec 1891; d.1989-Cubero, NM)

        sp: Felipe TRUJILLO

        Guadalupe ARMIJO (b.27 May 1894-Cubero, NM Terty)

    Vicenta GALLEGOS (b.30 Mar 1870-NM Terty)

    sp: Librado CHAVEZ (m.10 Nov 1885)

    Carmel GALLEGOS (b.11 Jul 1872-NM Terty)

    sp: Jose CHAVES (m.7 Nov 1890)

    Pedro GALLEGOS (b.28 feb 1875-NM Terty)

    Roberto GALLEGOS (b.15 Jun 1878-NM Terty)

    sp: Laurentia PINO (m.23 Nov 1897)

    sp: Paula RENTERIA (m.8 Jun 1916)

    Trinidad "Colorada" GALLEGOS (b.24 Oct 1880-NM Terty; d.1970s-McKinley Co, NM)

    Trinidad "La Apacha" ROMERO (b.27 Jun 1882-Cubero, NM Terty; d.8 Nov 1958-Cubero, NM)

    sp: Jose CHAVEZ (b.19 Sep 1872-Cubero, NM; m.27 Sep 1900)

        Marie CHAVEZ (b.Abt 1904)

        George CHAVEZ (b.Abt 1905)

        Estanislado CHAVEZ (b.Abt 1907)

    Carmel CHAVEZ (b.Abt 1909)
    David CHAVEZ (b.1913-Cubero, NM)
    Relles CHAVEZ (b.Abt 1918)
    Reyes CHAVEZ (b.14 Nov 1923-Cubero, NM; d.1998-Grants, NM)
    sp: Lina OTERO
      Sedencio CHAVEZ
      Beatrice CHAVEZ
    Plácida CHAVEZ (b.Oct 1933-Cubero, NM)
sp: Victor ROMERO (b.19 Jun 1862; m.14 Jan 1886)
   Bartola ROMERO (b.18 Nov 1891)
   Perfilio ROMERO (b.1 Jun 1894)

The dates above show that Plácida's first child, Felipa, was born about three years before Plácida and Domingo married and that Plácida was fifteen years old when they married and would have been twelve or thirteen at the time of Felipa's birth.

APPENDIX 4
Newspaper Articles on Plácida's Escape

RESCUED FROM THE APACHES

Two Citizens of New Mexico Escape From Their Indian Captors—
Five Others Yet in the Hands of the Hostiles

[Santa Fe] New Mexican Oct. 18 [1881]

The following information in regard to some children who were made captives by the Apaches during their recent raid in New Mexico, will be joyful news to the friends [of those] who have made their escape, but will only prolong the agony of those of the others who yet remain in the hands of the savages. It is also valuable as showing that the Mexican government is making strong efforts to drive the hostiles back this way and will enable the military authorities to prepare for them.

The following communication was received yesterday by Governor Sheldon from the Mexican consul at El Paso, in which he encloses the communication giving the news of the escape of the captives and a list of those who yet remain prisoners:

MEXICAN CONSULATE.
El Paso, Texas, Oct. 15, 1881.

To His Excellency, L. A. Sheldon, Governor of New Mexico:

Sir: - I have the honor to enclose you, herewith, a newspaper article which contains some information in regard to some children who were captured by the hostile Apache Indians of New Mexico. In regard to the two captives that were rescued from the Indians after the encounter in the Cañon del Cristo, I have already communicated with the Governor of the State of Chihuahua, who will probably advise me to deliver them over to their friends, and therefore they will do well to address me, in order that I may be able to return them to their families with all possible dispatch.

Please accept my highest considerations and respect.

(Sign'd) J. Escobary Armendaris.

The following letter was addressed to Mr. E. Medina, the editor of El Progresista, *a paper published in El Paso del Norte, and appeared in its columns in the issue of the 14th inst.:*

VALLE DE SAN BUENA VENTURA [Buenaventura], MEXICO,
September 30th, 1881.
Mr. E. Medina:

Dear Sir: Seeing the great interest you have taken to obtain from the Supreme Federal Government, the necessary means to defend our frontier from the continuous depredations of the hostile Indians and desiring to show that these Indians come from American Territory, I send you the following facts, hoping that you may see fit to give them publication:

On the 25th inst. about 6 o'clock A. M. the Indians attacked a farming ranch six miles west of this place called "La Casa del Llano" taking off with them several good horses. The civil authorities immediately set out in pursuit of the hostiles, sixty men well armed and mounted, headed by the chief authority at that place in person. Two hours after their departure they overtook the Indians in the "Cañon del Cristo," (Sierra Madre) where they were unable to recover the stock on account of the ruggedness of the mountains and the advantageous position of the Indians. Our people kept skirmishing with them for nine hours, and then determined to make an open attack. This was done and resulted in a loss of eight horses and the wounding of one man. A retreat was then made, without being able to ascertain the loss of the enemy.

One of the best results of the encounter, however, was: that near the place of the fight, two captives held by the Indians made good their escape and came to our camp. They are from Cubero, New Mexico, and their names are Placida Romero, a woman of thirty years of age, and a native of Cubero, N.M., who was captured on the 8th day of last August, while on a ranch called la Cebolla, and Probencio Garcia, a young boy nine years old from el Pueblo del Gallo, [San Rafael] N. M. From these captives we learned that the Indians are twelve in number who have their families with them; and that these Indians are the remainder of the famous Victorio band. Also that they are headed by Tato, a brother [*sic*] of Victorio, and that they have four more captives with them, most of whom are from New Mexico, whose names are: Telesforo Romero, Meliton ____, Concepcion ____, and Silvestre ____, whose ages are respectively, sixteen, twelve, nine and seven years. There is also another whose name they do not know, aged about fifteen years. They also informed us that the intention of Chief Tato is to turn his course towards Chihuahua, with the view of exchanging the captives for Indian captives, and that they are very well equipped with horses, arms and money, and ammunition. I believe you will do much good by publishing the names of the captives, and also of the rescue of the two in order to relieve the anxiety of their relatives and to enable them to know of their whereabouts.

Please be kind enough to publish this communication in your paper, if you deem it important enough. A. P. MATA.

The above articles were reprinted together on October 22, 1881, in the Las Cruces, New Mexico, newspaper, Río Grande Republican.

APPENDIX 5
Act of the Legislative Assembly of the Territory of New Mexico, 1882

1882.—PRIVATE LAWS OF NEW MEXICO.—25TH SESSION
CHAPTER CIII.

AN ACT FOR THE RANSOM AND TRANSPORTATION OF CERTAIN CITIZENS OF NEW MEXICO, WHO WERE CAPTURED BY THE NANE BAND OF APACHE INDIANS, ON THE TENTH DAY OF AUGUST, 1881, AND WHO ARE NOW IN THE REPUBLIC OF MEXICO.

CONTENTS.

SECTION 1. Authorizes such expenses as may be incurred in the return from Mexico of Placido Romero and Procopio Garcia, captured by Indians.

On the tenth day of August, A. D. 1881, a band of marauding Apache Indians, under the command of one certain Nane, on a pillaging and bloody campaign in the county of Valencia, and after having cruelly killed several citizens of said county, among which the principal were Domingo Gallegos, Jesus Maria Bargas, Timotes Baca, and Pedro [Pino] Molina, and they carried off captives certain citizens of this Territory; and

WHEREAS, Placida Romero, wife (widow) of the said Domingo Gallegos, deceased, and Procopio Garcia, adopted son of said deceased and Placida Romero, were ransomed from the hands of said Apache Indians by the military authorities of the Republic of Mexico. And,

WHEREAS, It is the imperative duty of the Territory of New Mexico to use its greatest exertions, not only to protect the people of New Mexico from the depredations of the savage Indians, but also to secure all the reparation possible for all the evils inflicted by Indian nations. Therefore,

Be it enacted by the Legislative Assembly of the Territory of New Mexico:

SECTION 1. That His Excellency, the Governor of the Territory of New Mexico be, and is hereby authorized and empowered to enter into correspondence with the authorities of the State of Chihuahua, or with any other State of the Republic of Mexico, for the purpose of ascertaining, if in case Placida Romero and Procopio Garcia are now in said Republic, and in case if one or both of them are there, that said Governor request that they be returned to the jurisdiction of this Territory, and for that purpose he be, and is hereby authorized to investigate and pay any reasonable expense that said Republic may have incurred in the premises. And for the purpose of paying said costs, as also any other that may be necessary to obtain the safe return of one or both of said persons to the Territory; said Governor is hereby authorized and empowered to draw his warrant in the name of the Territory of New Mexico for the sum of such expenses, which warrant shall be directed to the Territorial Auditor, and on his approval thereof, the Territorial Treasurer shall pay said sum out of any money in his hands, not otherwise appropriated.
SEC. 2. This act shall be in force and effect from and after its passage.

Approved January 28, 1882.
[Translated]

The above excerpt is from Acts of the Legislative Assembly of the Territory of New Mexico, twenty-fifth session: convened at the capital, at the City of Santa Fe, on Monday, the 2d day of January, 1882, and adjourned on Thursday, the 2d day of March, 1882 *(Santa Fe, NM: Chas. W. Greene, Public Printer), chapter 103, 192–93.*

APPENDIX 6
Newspaper Articles Pertaining to Navajo Agent Galen Eastman

The Crónica del Río Colorado *or* Red River Chronicle *was a short-lived small-town newspaper that was published from 1880 through 1882, first at San Lorenzo and then at San Hilario, New Mexico. These towns were in eastern San Miguel County close to present-day Conchas Dam, the sites now likely being under water. Edited and published by Louis Hommel, the paper was bilingual, publishing an English and Spanish edition weekly. Unaffiliated politically, the paper championed the small ranchers/homesteaders over the cattle barons/land grabbers and was adamantly opposed to the illegal fencing of public lands. The editor later changed the paper's name and moved it to Las Vegas, New Mexico, as a daily. These newspaper files are now housed at the University of New Mexico Zimmerman Library, Albuquerque. This information is from Porter A. Stratton,* The Territorial Press of New Mexico 1834–1912 *(Albuquerque: University of New Mexico Press, 1969), 161, 284.*

RED RIVER CHRONICLE 6 MAY 1882

Plácida Romero, whose husband Domingo Gallegos, was killed on the 8th day of August, 1881, and since which time she had been captive, being now returned home accuses the Navajoes to have helped the Apaches kill her husband and states that a certain Margarito, a Navajo, still keeps her child captive which she demands to have restored. She positively swears to the names of certain Navajoe Indians implicated in the murder of her husband and another man, his partner, and of abducting her child. Now let District Attorney Barnes move in the matter.

RED RIVER CHRONICLE 24 JUNE 1882
The Navajo Indians

In our last issue we published, on the Spanish side, a letter from Mr. Gregorio N. Otero, Cubero, in Valencia County, about the outrageous conduct of agent Galen Eastman. This thing ought to be investigated by proper authorities. There is a sworn statement in existence, already published in these columns formerly, where Plácida Romero names several Navajo Indians who helped the Apaches to kill her husband last year; steal her baby and take the woman captive into Old Mexico, where she was rescued. The Governor of New Mexico wanted to know something about the matter and sent the sworn declaration to Agent Eastman, to investigate. Because the Navajoes, accused of this crime, as is natural they would, refuse to criminate themselves in their testimony and deny the facts, as occurred, that scalawag of Eastman comes out and says the sworn statement of the woman is false and that the word of the accused Indians ought to be believed.

Of course Eastman wants to shield himself. He already reported his Indians at home and peaceful: if the statement of the woman is given credit it shows plainly that his reports were false; that he stole the rations of the absent Indians and that will prove him to be a perjured liar in making false reports and a thief of the public moneys. Is this thing to be dropped in this unsatisfactory manner? We advise our Valencia County friends to take the matter in their own hands.

Of course it would be unlawful to advise them to make that hypocrite Eastman suffer swift punishment; it is also against the laws of the country to tie him to a stake, cut off limb after limb and roast his dirty heart in his own body over a slow fire of green wood, but let them take the above mentioned sworn declaration of the woman Plácida Romero, gather up additional evidence of fraud of the scalawag Eastman and of depredations committed by the Navajoes and send the whole outfit of documentary evidence, one copy to the President of the United States and others to the Secretary of the Interior, Commissioner of Indian Affairs, presiding officers of both houses of Congress and the Delegate to Congress from New Mexico, calling for investigations of charges, punishment of the murderers, restoration of the child and the indictment of that thieving liar who is now the agent. Bring the matter to an issue, and redress to the poor widow.

RED RIVER CHRONICLE 1 JULY 1882

The scalawag Eastman says he is willing to open the door to investigation, and continues his assertion that the Apaches killed Plácida Romero's child, now who is to be believed? A loving mother, who saw one of the Navajoes carry away her little girl alive, to be kept a captive, or the accused Indian and his cowardly agent? The people are the jury and will render the verdict.

RED RIVER CHRONICLE 9 AUGUST 1882

An Indian Agents' Crime

Special Agent Howard, of the Indian Bureau, found out several things in connection with the management of Navajo Indian affairs, which Mr. Eastman would have preferred would have remained private. Mr. Eastman has, since he has been the agent of the Navajos, persistently reported to the bureau at Washington that all the Indians were on the reservation, with the exception now and then of a small hunting party. Inspector Howard found, upon examination, that over 8,000 Navajos were off the reservation some of whom had not been living within its line for two years. This is a contradiction which it will be very hard for Mr. Eastman to explain. Again, Mr. Eastman has frequently referred to the good effects of the policy of moral suasion he was using and to the influence he had over the Indians. While Inspector Howard was at Defiance the Navajos broke open and robbed the storehouse, and Mr. Eastman was impotent to prevent it. These are but two of the facts which the report of Inspector Howard will contain; there are others which will work equal disaster to Mr. Eastman's hope that he will be allowed to remain as an Indian agent longer. He has but a short time more as agent of the Navajos.
—*Albuquerque Review*

This is really too bad. After upholding these Indian Agents persistently as honest, pious men, gentlemen picked out by religious denomination for their Christian character and moral persuation, the Chronicle is forced to acknowledge to have been mistaken. Poor Eastman! Now he will have to get along on one ration, like other mortal sinners; after having got used to big feasts of 8,000 daily rations. Too bad.

Lamentably, this was the second time Galen Eastman had been appointed Navajo Indian Agent. The following is quoted from the Las Cruces newspaper, Río Grande Republican, *August 13, 1881, almost exactly a year earlier.*

Eastman and the Navajos

Reports of trouble brewing among the Navajo Indians still continue to circulate and it seems likely that it may culminate in a revolt after all. It all comes of the reinstatement of Galen Eastman as agent. A little more than a year ago the Navajoes made it so hot for Eastman that he was forced to leave the agency for safety and take refuge in Albuquerque, where he loafed about on full pay for several months. Capt. Bennett of the U. S. Army was made the temporary agent and all trouble ceased. Eastman was advised by all interested to resign, it having been fully demonstrated that he was not the man for the place, but he was not of the resigning kind. He is a brother-in-law of Senator Ferry of Michigan and an office must be provided for him, regardless of his qualifications. If he is incapable of performing the duties of the office, he must have the pay anyhow.

During Capt. Bennett's administration absolute peace and quiet reigned on the reservation except in a few instances where whiskey was smuggled in and sold to the Indians. Now the Department reinstates Eastman and the trouble again begins and assumes a worse shape if possible than before. Why was Eastman returned to the agency since he had proven a failure after ample trial? Must the lives of hundreds of good people be indangered to give Mr. Ferry's brother-in-law an office? The Secretary of Interior can certainly have no opinion of his own in this matter.

The people whose lives are thus placed in jeopardy should be heard as to whether this powerful savage Indian tribe shall be placed under a person who can possibly incite a revolt.

APPENDIX 7
Albuquerque Daily Journal Articles

11 AUGUST 1881 [LAGUNA]

Apaches reported in force about 15 miles south of Acoma. Five men reported killed; a number missing. An Acoma Indian who was reported captured yesterday afternoon, and escaped, said the Apaches told him they were moving in two groups, one to strike west of McCartys and the other east of Laguna. Renegade Navajos with them. Sent out 60 Laguna scouts last night, 40 of them mounted. No report as yet. Furnished R. R. men at El Rito, 20 stands of arms and ammunition. To Saulpaugh's men 80 guns and rounds of ammunition. Have 20 men at Laguna. Detachment in each of the other villages. Above reported to the Journal by W. G. Marmon. (*Albuquerque Daily Journal*)

W. G. (Walter Gunn) Marmon was the brother of Robert Gunn Marmon who was the grandfather of Leland (Lee) Marmon, the well-known photographer from Laguna Pueblo, New Mexico, whose photographs appear in this book.

12 AUGUST 1881 [MCCARTYS STATION]

Currier from Cebolla Springs brings this report to McCartys station. Lt. Guilfoil and myself arrived here last night. Found two men dead and women carried off. Captain Parker is at Alamosa. Lt. Thomas had two fights recently. Hostiles between Cebolla and Dátil Mountains. Suggest send troops to Mónica and Suera to head them off. [Undoubtedly this refers to the Luera Springs and Mountains southwest of Mónica Springs, a known Indian hunting campground.] Francisco Duran of Cubero is here with Mexicans without arms and asks to loan him some for which he will be responsible. Wants to follow Apaches. Lt. Guilfoil has 27 men. I have 15.
   Signed, Harry Wright, Lt. 9th Cavalry
27 soldiers under Capt. McArthur arrived last night. Will follow Wrights instructions. Indians known to be all around. (*Albuquerque Daily Journal*)

The location of the "Alamosa" in the above dispatch is uncertain. A military post at Cañada Alamosa sat close to present-day Monticello, New Mexico, but it was too distant for Captain Parker to have engaged the Indians from there on 12 August as was reported. Historian Jerry D. Thompson in Desert Tiger: Captain

Paddy Graydon and the Civil War in the Far Southwest locates Cañada Alamosa on the west bank of the Río Grande at the mouth of Alamosa Creek, over one hundred miles away. Another possibility is an old military outpost located on the Alamocita Creek. Since all old references call the Alamocita Creek "Alamosa," it is likely this outpost (improved military encampment area) is the location referred to in the dispatch. This site is only some thirty miles west of the Carrizo Canyon/Ciénega Ranch battle area. The location of this military station was made known to me through interviews with a local area rancher, and military equipment has been seen at this site by this author. This location would have been well within Captain Parker's range for the August 12 engagement near Carrizo Canyon and was certainly the encampment used by Army troops patrolling the Río Salado and Red Canyon area of the Dátils for rampaging Indians. The site contains four well-made, widely spaced stone buildings: a small stores house/shop; a multiroom mess building with officers' quarters; a small stable shed; and a possible guard house at the main entrance. The area was fenced, with a large space between the buildings that could be used as a tent encampment for the troops and corrals for the mounts. The area is sited on a rise that gives clear views in all directions, and there is evidence of a guard post on a higher rise overlooking the whole enclosure area. A reference book, *New Mexico Frontier Military Place Names* by Daniel C. B. Rathbun and David B. Alexander notes: "French, Camp ------ The exact location of this camp is unknown, but it was probably named for Lieutenant James Hansel French, 9th U.S. Cavalry, who was killed by the Ojo Caliente Apaches in the San Mateo Mts. on 17 January 1880. ------In *The Conquest of Apacheria*, written in 1967, author Dan Thrapp places the camp on the Alamosa River." This author believes the location "at Alamosa" in the dispatch refers to the former Camp French located on Alamocita Creek, then known as "Alamosa." This location is mislabeled on present-day Geological Survey maps as the "Box Bar Place." The Box Bar brand belonged to Lawrence Parsons and family who homesteaded on Alamosa (Alamocita) Creek in 1908. Their former place is well known to be farther down the Alamocita by about a mile than as marked on the maps, and the descriptions of the Parsons' place do not fit the ruins that are visible there now (information from Mike McWhorter, a rancher born in this vicinity). Some military historians do not agree with the author's conclusion that this is actually the location of former Camp French, but I believe in the future it will be confirmed. To the author's knowledge, no military description of the location has been found, to date, in any archives.

The Luera Springs site is now on private ranch property providing water for ranch operations with no general access for unauthorized persons. A tour provided by the owner revealed evidence of heavy Apache and Navajo seasonal usage in the 1800s. Wickiup foundations and many stone arrow points are visible here.

This site had also been improved by the military in the 1870s with the construction of two large stone reservoirs to impound the water from the springs. It was utilized as an overnight and watering stop on the supply wagon route from Fort Craig to Fort Tularosa.

12 AUGUST 1881 MCCARTYS

Our party with Capt. McArthur are enroute from Laguna to Grants and Fort Wingate, where Apaches are likely to pass, northwest. El Rito Mexicans with Laguna scouts are 30 miles south of Laguna on hot trail of Apaches, who are reported divided.

    Soldiers from Ingalls and Shaeffers are in Laguna this morning conferring with the Marmon brothers. Expect Indians at Cubero today. They are hard pressed from the south. (*Albuquerque Daily Journal*)

14 AUGUST 1881 SOCORRO 4 P.M.

Indians struck a wagon train loaded for the Black Range yesterday morning. Killed two: further on killed Juan Dios Baca and his son, within 7 miles of Socorro. At night they struck Werner's ranch [approximately twenty seven miles south of Socorro], killed him and captured his wife, and 25 miles northwest killed three Mexicans. 30 Mexicans after them. (*Albuquerque Daily Journal*)

APPENDIX 8
Las Cosas Perdidas de Rancho Armijo: Analysis of Artifacts Recovered from the Homestead of Antonio and Manuela Armijo in the Los Pilares Valley, New Mexico

Carol A. Macaulay-Jameson, MA, RPA

INTRODUCTION

Manuela Gallegos Romero was the daughter of Domingo Gallegos and Plácida Romero. When she was 13 years old, her father was brutally killed by an Apache war party and her mother and youngest sibling were taken captive. A ballad memorializing the event and its aftermath was written for and performed by Plácida's family over a hundred years ago. Forty years of research by A. E. "Bob" Roland and Arthur G. Bibo has brought this story back to life. The "story," as Bob likes to call it, provides a glimpse into the daily lives of the farmers, ranchers, and trade folk who labored to make a living during the last decades of the nineteenth century in west-central New Mexico.

There was another connection these historians had to this family. It was Manuela, or Manuelita, as she was often called. Sometime after the turn of the century, Manuela and her husband, Antonio Armijo, homesteaded the land on which Arthur Bibo established his ranch headquarters in 1942. It was this land that he then sold to Bob Roland in 1971.[1] This report describes the *cosas perdidas encontrado* (small things found) during an archaeological survey in 2010 and 2014.

THE ARMIJO FAMILY

When Antonio Armijo and Manuela Gallegos Romero were married in 1883, he was 25 years old and she was 15. He had been working as a laborer in San Rafael, a small village south of Grants. Manuela was living with her family in Cubero, east of Grants at that time.[2] By 1900, Antonio and Manuela had four children. Margarita was 13, Beneranda was 11, Rosa was 8, and Guadalupe was 7. According to the 1900 Census, the family was living in a rented house in Jaralosa (Jaralozo), southwest of Grants, where Antonio was employed as a teamster.[3] According to Richard L. Nostrand in *The Hispano Homeland*, Cubero families began moving to the Jaralosa Canyon area in the 1880s.[4] Sometime during the first decade of the twentieth century, Antonio and Manuela relocated to the Cebollita Canyon area and purchased 260 acres of land in Los Pilares Valley.[5] The 1910 Census lists Antonio's profession as a cattleman and he carried no mortgage on his ranch. All the children had moved away by this time.[6]

THE INVESTIGATION

Archaeological Features

During the summer of 2010, an archaeological survey was conducted on the property. Of particular interest are inscriptions painted (pictographs) and etched (petroglyphs) on a vertical face of a sandstone hoodoo located on the property. Three initials "J.L.A." and the date "1916" had been painted on this face. These inscriptions may represent the initials of one of the members of the Armijo extended family. The 1910 Census lists one other family with the surname Armijo living in the vicinity.[7] This family, headed by José Armijo, 35, and wife, Carolina, 28, had six children, ages 5 through 17. Their youngest son was named Antonio. This family may have been relatives of Antonio Armijo. José's profession was listed as a sheepherder, and he may have been in business with Antonio. José may have painted his initials on the sandstone during a visit to the Armijo ranch in 1916. Located on the formation were two petroglyphs. One is an underscored capital letter "A" with the number "4" below ("A Bar 4") and the other is a capital letter "A" encased by a circle ("Circle A"). These were probably livestock brands belonging to the Armijo family.[8]

Three additional features are all that remains of the farmstead where this family spent much of their working lives: a circular pile of sandstone rocks which may have once been part of a cistern; a linear formation of cut sandstone rocks which may represent a door threshold; and eleven juniper posts, forming a circular corral with a snubbing post in the center, approximately twelve meters in diameter. In addition to these features, the farmstead most likely contained a log residence, a number of sheds, a chicken coop, a root cellar, a windmill and well, an outhouse, additional corrals, and garden plots.

Cosas perdidas (artifacts)

Almost two hundred historic artifacts were collected and analyzed. All date from the last decades of the nineteenth century through the first decades of the twentieth century. They represent glass bottles and jars, utilitarian stoneware vessels, refined earthenware, and semi-porcelain tablewares, windowpane glass, metal can fragments, personal items and ammunition.

More than one-half of the artifact assemblage consisted of bottle-glass fragments, one-third of which were made from aqua-colored glass, the dominant color of bottle glass of the nineteenth century. One-half of the bottle-glass fragments represent bottles manufactured with manganese dioxide, a decolorizing agent used to produce clear bottle glass during the late 1880s through 1920. When this glass was exposed to sunlight, it turned an amethyst color.[9] Amber (brown) and clear bottle-glass fragments represent approximately fifteen percent of the assemblage. Most of the body fragments are thick, suggesting that they were part of bottles that held carbonated beverages such as beer or soda.

All of the bottle-base fragments recovered represent bottles that were mouth blown into cup-bottom molds, the most common type of mold used from the mid-1880s through 1910.[10] The majority of the aqua-colored lip/neck bottle fragments exhibit double-ring or extract tooled finishes, indicating that a lipping tool was used to form the bottle lip. This tool was used from the 1890s through the 1910s.[11] These finishes were commonly used on rectangular medicine bottles that once had paper labels. One panel fragment embossed with the script "*Fleche__*" represents a Fletcher's Castoria bottle. Fletcher's Castoria, patented in 1868, was not a castor oil, but a laxative composed of senna, sodium bicarbonate, essence of wintergreen, sugar, and water.[12] The Armijo family most likely purchased medicinal products from mercantile establishments in Cubero or Grants. Fragments representing two small milk-glass jars with external threads were also recovered. Milk glass was most commonly used for cosmetic and toiletry jars and dates from the 1870s to about 1920.[13]

Three wide-mouth bottle finishes, decolorized with manganese dioxide, used to hold food products, were also recovered on the property. The first exhibits a capseat or milk-bottle finish. This style of finish was patented in 1889 but was not widely used until the early-1900s.[14] This find suggests that a commercial dairy was operating in the vicinity. The second finish exhibiting an extract finish, possibly held pickles or olives. The third represents a canning jar with external threads and a ground rim which dates its manufacture to before 1910.[15] The Armijo family had the means to purchase "store-bought" condiments, but they also canned fruits and vegetables growing in their garden.

Before the advent of refrigeration, durable and economical stoneware crockery was used to hold butter and lard, salted meats, and pickled vegetables. The Armijo family owned a number of different-sized stoneware jars, one of which is represented by a rim sherd exhibiting a recessed shelf to support a lid. The mouth of this jar was ten inches in diameter. All but one of the stoneware sherds were decorated with a combination of Albany (brown) and Bristol (whitish-gray) slips, both of which were common at the turn of the twentieth century.[16]

The majority of the tablewares used by the Armijo family were undecorated whitewares and semi-porcelains. However, a few of their tablewares were decorated. Decalware was first introduced in 1890 and involved the application of a polychrome decal under or over the glaze. Four whiteware sherds representing a large plate were decorated with under-glaze decals of pink and red flowers, green leaves, and sprigs. Two semi-porcelain sherds were decorated with over-glaze decals of purple and white flowers and green leaves, and represent a small plate.

A semi-porcelain twelve-inch dinner plate imprinted on the bottom with "Made in Germany" fits well within the time frame of the Armijo's residency. In 1891, the United States passed the McKinley Tariff Act, which required manufacturers from all over the world to mark products for export to the United States.[17] The Armijos owned at least three complete or incomplete sets of tablewares, represented by whiteware and semi-porcelain fragments of six-, eight-, and twelve-inch diameter plates, bowls, and teacups, as well as an undecorated semi-porcelain sugar bowl.

Windowpane glass fragments ranging in thickness from 1.8 mm to 2.4 mm were also recovered. Window glass gradually increased in thickness throughout the nineteenth century and beyond. Using Randall Moir's glass thickness dating method, the majority of these fragments date to the first two decades of the twentieth century, suggesting that Antonio had to replace broken windowpanes quite often.[18]

The top portion of a 9/16 inch-diameter brass shank button with the script "Jumbo Make" and embossed image of an elephant was also recovered. This button dates from 1910–1920 and was used on work clothes such as bib-overalls.[19]

A number of cartridges were also recovered on the property. One is a brass cartridge imprinted with "U.M.C. No. 12 Nitro Club." This .12-gauge shotgun cartridge was made by the Union Metallic Cartridge Co. before it merged with Remington in 1912. A centerfire copper cartridge was imprinted with "45 Colt WRA Co." This .45 cartridge was manufactured by the Winchester Repeating Arms Co. & Colt Mfg. Co., which used this head stamp until 1928.[20]

One of the most unique artifacts was found by Bob Roland. It was a fragment of the right side of the face of a bisque doll. The fragment was tinted pink and has finely painted lower eyelashes. Bisque dolls were an innovation in the late-1860s because they were more life-like in appearance. Up to that time, dolls were made of glazed white porcelain. Bisque dolls had leather, cloth, or composition bodies. Most bisque dolls were first imported from France, and then in the late 1800s, Germany exported the most to the United States.[21] This doll may have once belonged to one of Antonio and Manuela's daughters.

CONCLUSION

After the Civil War, Americans began moving to the Territory of New Mexico and so did their material culture. A significant part of this growth began with the arrival of the railroads. In 1881, the Atlantic and Pacific Railroad was completed from Albuquerque to Gallup.[22] By 1897, this railroad and others became part of the Atchison, Topeka and Santa Fe, serving the agricultural, livestock, mining, and timber industries.[23] These railroads also supplied merchants with medicinal products, toiletries, canned and bottled foods, alcohol, carbonized beverages, kitchen and household wares, toys, guns, and ammunition, manufactured in the United

States and beyond. During this time, at least eighty-seven Hispano communities had one German Jewish merchant who sold and bartered their merchandize for the wool and sheep of the local farmers and ranchers.[24] One of these merchants was Emil Bibo. In 1910, Emil, 48, and his wife Elizabeth, 40, were the proprietors of a mercantile establishment in Cubero. They had three children, Irma, 12; Arthur, 11; and Philip, 7.[25] It is not too far-fetched to imagine Arthur loading a wagon of household supplies, including necessities such as a case of Remington cartridges, canning jars, and new windowpanes into Antonio's wagon one Saturday morning. It is even possible to imagine Manuela purchasing a bottle of Fletcher's Castoria, a jar of cold cream, or a new set of tableware ordered by Emil from a German supplier. Imagine Antonio treating his family to cold, carbonized sodas before heading back to the ranch.

A hundred years pass and Bob Roland finds the face of a late nineteenth-century German china doll on his Los Pilares Valley ranch—a small memento of Plácida Romero's legacy.

BIBLIOGRAPHY

AntiqueMarks.com. "What Are Antique Marks?," 2021. https://antique-marks.com/antique-marks.html.

Christopher, Catherine. *The Complete Book of Doll Making and Collecting.* New York: Dover Publications, 1971.

Greer, Georgeanna H. *American Stonewares: The Art and Craft of Utilitarian Potters.* Exton, PA: Schiffer Publishing Limited, 1981.

Kowalski, David D., ed. *Standard Catalog of Winchester: The Most Comprehensive Price Guide Ever Published.* Iola, WI: Krause Publications, 2000.

Lindsey, Bill. "Bottle Bases." Historic Glass Bottle Identification and Information Website, Society for Historical Archaeology, 2021. https://sha.org/bottle/bases.htm.

———. "Bottle/Glass Colors." Society for Historical Archaeology, 2020. https://sha.org/bottle/colors.

———. "Bottle Finishes (aka 'Lips') and Closures." Society for Historical Archaeology, 2020. https://sha.org/bottle/finishes.htm.

———. "Bottle Typing/Diagnostic Shapes, Food Bottles and Canning Jars." Society for Historical Archaeology, 2021. https://sha.org/bottle/food.htm.

Lockhart, Bill, Beau Schreiver, Carol Serr, and Bill Lindsey. "Pitcher's and Fletcher's Castoria, An Uncommon Study of Common Bottles." In *Encyclopedia of Manufacturers Marks on Glass Containers*. Society for Historical Archaeology, 2019. https://sha.org/bottle/pdffiles/CastoriaHistory.pdf.

Myrick, David F. *New Mexico's Railroads: A Historical Survey*. Albuquerque: University of New Mexico Press, 1990.

Nostrand, Richard Lee. *The Hispano Homeland*. Norman: University of Oklahoma Press, 1996.

PicClick.com. "Antique Brass Work Clothes Overall Button 'Jumbo Make' w/ Elephant - 11/16 in.," 2021. https://picclick.com/Antique-Brass-Work-Clothes-Overall-Button-Jumbo-Make-382468936625.html.

US Bureau of the Census. "1880 Population, New Mexico, Valencia County, San Rafael, District 054." Heritage Quest Online, Baylor University Libraries, Waco, TX. https://www.ancestryheritagequest.com/imageviewer/collections/6742/images/4242011-00716?usePUB=true&_phsrc=dBp20&_phstart=successSource&usePUBJs=true&pId=43409254.

———. "1900 Population, New Mexico, Valencia County, Jaralozo, District 0175." Heritage Quest Online, Baylor University Libraries, Waco, TX. https://www.ancestryheritagequest.com/imageviewer/collections/7602/images/4120507_00907?usePUB=true&_phsrc=dBp25&_phstart=successSource&usePUBJs=true&pId=48325162.

———. "1910 Population, New Mexico, Valencia County, Cubero, District 0287." Heritage Quest Online, Baylor University Libraries, Waco, TX. https://www.ancestryheritagequest.com/imageviewer/collections/7884/images/31111_4330942-00979?usePUB=true&_phsrc=dBp28&_phstart=successSource&usePUBJs=true&pId=16936521.

———. "1910 Population, New Mexico, Valencia County, San Rafael, District 0292." Heritage Quest Online, Baylor University Libraries, Waco, TX. https://www.ancestryheritagequest.com/imageviewer/collections/7884/images/31111_4330942-01127?backlabel=ReturnSearchResults&queryId=294ea7cd9ed936babddee84e2cea7444&pId=16938239.

———. "1910 Population, New Mexico, Valencia County, Valencia, District 0289." Heritage Quest Online, Baylor University Libraries, Waco, TX. https://www.ancestryheritagequest.com/imageviewer/collections/7884/images/31111_4330942-01041?backlabel=ReturnSearchResults&queryId=b3c168f71157ea70f118ccb215e072d0&pId=16937166.

Van Patten, Denise. "Introduction to Bisque and Porcelain Dolls," 2019. https://www.thesprucecrafts.com/bisque-and-porcelain-dolls-774692.

Venovcevs, Antolijs. *Dress for Life and Death: The Archaeology of Common Nineteenth-Century Buttons*. Toronto: Archaeological Services Inc., 2013.

Weiland, Jonathan. "A Comparison and Review of Window Glass Analysis Approaches in Historical Archaeology." *Technical Briefs in Historical Archaeology* 4, no. 2 (2009): 29–40.

Wikipedia. "Gallup, New Mexico," 2021. https://en.wikipedia.org/wiki/Gallup,_New_Mexico.

NOTES AND HISTORICAL COMMENTARY

INTRODUCTION by Enrique R. Lamadrid

1. Amy Shuman, "Entitlement and Empathy in Personal Narrative," *Narrative Inquiry* 16, no. 1 (2006): 149.

2. *NM Legislative Journal CIII*, January 28, 1882.

3. *Crónica del Río Colorado*, June 10, 1882.

CORRIDO DE PLÁCIDA ROMERO

1. Enrique R. Lamadrid, "La Pasión de Plácida Romero: The Poetics of Faith, Authority, and Remembrance of a Cautiva and her Ballad" (unpublished manuscript, December 2010), hard copy.

2. This information on the composition of the ballad came from Rosa Trujillo, granddaughter of Plácida (Rosa Trujillo interviews with Arty Bibo, summer 1966, Albuquerque, NM; October 17, 1969, Albuquerque, NM; December 3, 1969, Cubero, NM). Some other members of the family think the ballad was written by Calletano Romero, brother of Plácida. In fact, there is a version of the ballad probably written by Calletano. That version is markedly different from the original, particularly in the number of stanzas per verse and the lack of rhyming of the stanzas. However, many words and expressions are the same or similar, although this alternate version is considerably shorter, having only seven verses. This may have been Calletano's version of what he remembered of the original. This is also the version for which the music has been discovered.

3. Although this phrase "el tato" is not capitalized in the original ballad, in Spanish it is often used as a nickname for "grandfather." It is now known that "tato" was indeed used as a nickname for the leader of the Indians in the raiding party, which was Nana himself (*Río Grande Republican*, October 22, 1881).

4. The actual date of the murders, as related in a deposition given by Plácida to Gregorio N. Otero of Cubero, was August 8, 1881. This deposition was published in the *Red River Chronicle* on May 13, 1882, in the Spanish edition. Because the whole occurrence happened to coincide with Día de San Lorenzo, the celebration of the patron saint of Cubero on August 10, that is the date used in the ballad.

5. Plácida's mother was María Acacia Gonzales. An error in transcription is probably responsible for the shorter name Cacia. In some other versions of the ballad, it appears as Marucasia. Other spellings in church records appear as Eufrasia, Eucasia, and Eucarsia.

6. Plácida talks here of "that burning pain." This may well have been a physical as well as an emotional pain, since she was forced to give up her nursing nine-month-old daughter a dozen or so miles back, at Blue Water Vega, close to Mesa de la Escoba.

7. This line is Plácida's plea to the patronal Virgen of Cubero, Nuestra Señora de la Luz. The Catholic Church in Cubero is still named "Our Lady of Light."

8. Manuelita was Plácida's second eldest daughter, who went to Cubero with her uncle the day before the killings at Rancho Cebolla. Felipa was Plácida's oldest daughter; reported as being fifteen years old in the 1880 Census, Felipa was three years older than Manuelita. In the church records for September 24, 1883, Manuelita and Felipa were reported as marrying on the same day. Felipa's marriage record states she was the daughter of both Domingo and Plácida; however, her birth date precedes the marriage date of her parents by approximately three years. Some family members surmise Felipa was actually raised by other members of the extended family, and this could very well be true. Plácida would have been twelve or thirteen years old at the time of Felipa's delivery and possibly would not have been prepared to be a mother.

9. The last two lines in this verse are reproduced as they occur in the original text. However, this order appears to be a transcription error, for they should be switched to preserve the rhyme scheme of the ballad in Spanish. In accordance with this verse, and as reported by Anna Mae Starr (A. M. Starr to A. Bibo, October 13, 1970, author's collection), Plácida and Domingo's other children were cared for by Plácida's father Pedro Molina Romero, with her brother Calletano, supplying the provisions while their mother was captive in Mexico.

10. The date September 25, 1881, was obviously an important one to Plácida. We now know that was the date that she actually escaped from her captivity (*Río Grande Republican*, October 22, 1881). Plácida was enslaved by the Apaches for forty-nine days, slightly less than two months.

11. Sierra Cristo is the mountain group in the Sierra Madre range northwest of Buenaventura, Mexico, that contains Cañón del Cristo, the location where Nana's group of raiders took some stolen horses while they were being chased by the Mexican authorities and where Plácida was given the opportunity to escape by the Apache women.

12. Even after they had been notified of Plácida's whereabouts, more than six months passed before her family in Cubero could begin the trip to repatriate Plácida. This phrase seems to be an expression of sorrow. Does she feel her family has abandoned her? This verse could also refer to the time, after Plácida returned, when she realized she would not be able to retrieve her daughter, Trinidad, from the Navajos.

CHAPTER I. BACKGROUND

1. Floyd S. Fierman, *Guts and Ruts: The Jewish Pioneer on the Trail in the American Southwest* (New York: KTAV Publishing House, 1985), 58.

2. Felipe Trujillo and Rosenda "Rosa" Trujillo were married May 19, 1918, in the church of Saint Joseph in Winslow, Arizona. Reverend Ed Albany officiated at the service with the witnesses being Igínio Maestas and Piedád Maestas. This information is from Rosa Trujillo, interview by Arty Bibo, Albuquerque, New Mexico, October 17, 1969, in possession of the author.

3. The note accompanying the gift of the ballad reads as follows: "Original Corrido of Plácida Romero given to Arthur Bibo Oct. 1, 1969, by Rosa Trujillo. The original copy. [Signed] Rosa Trujillo."

4. Stephen H. Lekson, *Nana's Raid: Apache Warfare in Southern New Mexico, 1881* (El Paso: Texas Western Press, 1987), 22. Another apparent misjudgment was that Nana's party crossed the US-Mexico border with Plácida into the Mexican state of Sonora instead of Chihuahua (Lekson, *Nana's Raid*, 32).

5. The volumes consulted concerning the activities of the Buffalo Soldiers related to this story are: William H. Leckie, *The Buffalo Soldiers: A Narrative of the Negro Cavalry in the West* (Norman: University of Oklahoma Press, 1967); Monroe L. Billington, *New Mexico's Buffalo Soldiers, 1866–1900* (Niwot: University Press of Colorado, 1991); Charles L. Kenner, *Buffalo Soldiers and Officers of the Ninth Cavalry 1867–1898* (Norman: University of Oklahoma Press, 1999); and Frank N. Schubert, *Voices of the Buffalo Soldier* (Albuquerque: University of New Mexico Press, 2003).

6. From Abe Peña, "Cíbola History: The Heritage of Los Alamitos," *Cíbola County Beacon* (Grants, NM), September 26, 2008, 8A.

7. This information on Bandelier's adventures is paraphrased from Bandelier's journal entries as related in Charles H. Lange and Carroll L. Riley, eds., *The Southwestern Journals of Adolph F. Bandelier 1880–1882* (Albuquerque: University of New Mexico Press, 1966), 297–305.

CHAPTER 2. THE TRAGIC CAPTURE OF PLÁCIDA ROMERO

1. Plácida Romero and Domingo Gallegos were married January 7, 1868. Officiated by J. B. Courbon at the church of Nuestra Señora de Los Dolores (Seboyeta, New Mexico). Witnesses were Negro Sarracino and José Antonio Sarracino. Information from Edward J. Schoolcraft et al., *Sacramental Records from the Archives of the Diocese of Gallup* (Albuquerque, NM: Hispanic Genealogical Research Center, 2002), 152.

2. According to the 1880 US Census for Cubero, Valencia County, New Mexico, June 9, 1880, 36, Plácida and Domingo's children and ages were: Felipa, 15 (daughter); Manuela, 12 (daughter); Vicenta, 10 (daughter); Carmel, 9 (daughter); Pedro, 5 (son); Roberto (also seen as Luverto, Luperto, or Loberto), 2 (son). Trinidad was not yet born as of the 1880 census and Plácida was listed as 28, Domingo as 40. The 1870 census lists Domingo as 25, making him 35 in 1880. Family genealogy records lead me to believe the 1870 census age is correct.

3. Captain Charles Parker to Assistant Adjutant General of the US Army, Santa Fe, NM/Fort Leavenworth, KS, August 12, 1881, via Socorro, New Mexico. Copy of telegram, Letters Received by the Office of the Adjutant General Main Series 1881–1889, File 4746, Adjutant General's Office 1881, Roll 44, Microcopy 689, Records of the Adjutant General's Office, Record Group 94 (Washington, DC: National Archives and Records Administration [NARA]), 1985.

4. Clay W. Vaden, *Mexican Boy Captured by Apache Indians* (Pioneer Story from the WPA Writer's Project, 1936–40), 1936. In 1936, Clay W. Vaden, an author who worked in the WPA Writers' Project, recorded an oral interview with Felipe Padilla, a resident of Quemado, an incident entitled *Mexican Boy Captured by Apache Indians*. Included in this interview was the following information. "In 1881 a band of Apaches . . . made their way to Las Cebollas (Onions) Rancho, owned by Tiburasio Caroin [or possibly Caron—probably a French Basque], north of Quemado. There the Indians murdered two more men and captured a young woman, Plasida [*sic*], August 10th [*sic*], 1881." This indicates that Rancho Cebolla was not owned by Domingo Gallegos. The most definitive description of the partidos system encountered by this author is in William J. Parish, *The Charles Ilfeld Company: A Study of the Rise and Decline of Mercantile Capitalism in New Mexico* (Cambridge, MA: Harvard University Press, 1961), 150–173.

5. Some sources refer to him as José María Morales, Jesús María Bargas, and Juan María Barga. I use José María Vargas in this story for three reasons. The first two names of this man, José María, are used in the original transcription of the ballad and his last name, Vargas, is used in a story published on this subject by Anna Mae Starr in *La Herencia del Norte*; but most significantly this nomenclature appears

in Plácida's affidavit of her captivity. Anna Mae Starr, "Plácida Romero: La Cautiva," *La Herencia del Norte*, Summer 1999: 14–15.

6. Here I rely on Eve Ball's extensive publications on the Apache Indians for the spelling of "Mangus" and "Mangas Coloradas," For example: Eve Ball, *In the Days of Victorio: Recollections of a Warm Springs Apache* (Tucson: University of Arizona Press, 1970); and Eve Ball, *Indeh: An Apache Odyssey* (Provo, UT: Brigham Young University Press, 1980). Also, na-NEH is the generally accepted pronunciation of Nana since many early references spelled the name Nané (Spanish version), Naneh, Naney, or Nanéy, according to Harold Miller, "Nana's Raid of 1881," *Password* 19, no. 2 (Summer 1974): 69. Warm Springs Apaches are also known as Ojo Caliente Apaches, Gileño or Gila Apaches, Mimbreño or Mimbres Apaches, Coppermine Apaches, and in their own tongue Tcihene (among other spellings), the "red paint people," the easternmost band of Chiricahuas.

CHAPTER 3. THE FLIGHT TO MEXICO

1. This is the ranch country that belonged to Carl Wilson in the 1970s, Seis and Wilson before, and now is the Bar 15 Ranch owned and operated by the Acoma Land and Cattle Company. The ranch was originally established by Kenneth Gunn in about 1900, the headquarters being located just north of Gunn Mesa, named after the family.

2. Lekson, *Nana's Raid*, 22; and Gary L. Tietjen, *Encounter with the Frontier* (Los Alamos, NM: self-published, 1969), 62. The ruins of the Rancho García main house are still visible today, although it took an airplane ride to find them. An intriguing discovery was made during this investigation. On a hill somewhat to the north of the ranch house, a tall cross, about ten feet high, has been erected. This cross may have been installed as a memorial to the family that was massacred here by Nana's raiders. This land is now part of Laguna Pueblo and is fenced off.

3. John M. Gunn, *Schat-Chen: History, Traditions and Narratives of the Queres Indians of Laguna and Acoma* (Albuquerque, NM: Albright & Anderson, 1917), 60, 62.

4. *Río Grande Republican*, August 20, 1881 (microfilm, New Mexico State Library, Santa Fe).

5. See Agnes Morely Cleaveland, *No Life for a Lady* (Boston: Houghton Mifflin Co., 1941), 32, 61, 71; Susan E. Lee, *These Also Served* (Los Lunas, NM: self-published, 1960), 38–39, 41–42; Ben W. Kemp, *Cow Dust and Saddle Leather* (Norman: University of Oklahoma Press, 1968), 225, 230; Langford R. Johnston, *Old Magdalena Cow Town* (Albuquerque, NM: Cottonwood Printing Co.,

1983), 45, 87; and a 1900 edition New Mexico map by Rand McNally and Company, and other sources too numerous to list. The US Geological Survey changed the name here to avoid confusion with another Alamosa Creek that heads on the west side of the San Mateo Mountains some forty-five miles to the south and empties into the Río Grande (now Elephant Butte Reservoir) south of the San Mateos.

6. The best work on the Alamo Navajos is David W. Adams, *Three Roads to Magdalena* (Lawrence: University Press of Kansas, 2016), 11–16. Also, Robert Julyan, *The Place Names of New Mexico* (Albuquerque: University of New Mexico Press, 1998), 8.

7. Lekson, *Nana's Raid*, 43.

8. Capt. Parker to Asst. Adjt. General of the Army, August 12, 1881. Letters Received by the Office of the Adjutant General Main Series 1881–1889, NARA.

9. Among other sources, this information was related to the author by Norman Cleaveland (son of Agnes Morley Cleaveland) at his ranch in Dátil Canyon on September 29, 1979. See also Johnston, *Old Magdalena Cow Town*, 45.

10. Apparently two different Ygnacio or Ignacio Bacas were killed during Nana's raid. One died on Alamocita Creek on August 6 or 7; see Gilberto Espinosa and Tibo J. Chávez, *El Río Abajo* (Pampa, TX: Pampa Print Shop, 1965), 173. The other was killed near Socorro on August 14, 1881; documented in the ballad and in the *Albuquerque Daily Journal* 1, no. 246, August 15, 1881 (Center for Southwest Research, University Libraries, University of New Mexico, Albuquerque).

CHAPTER 4. IN MEXICO AND RETURN HOME

1. Col. Hatch to Gen. Pope and Adjt. Gen. of the US Army, August 23, 1881. Letters Received by the Office of the Adjutant General Main Series 1881–1889, NARA.

2. Charles F. Lummis, *General Crook and the Apache Wars* (Flagstaff, AZ: Northland Press, 1966), 133.

3. William Cochran McGaw, *Savage Scene* (New York: Hastings House, 1972; reprint, San Lorenzo, NM: High-Lonesome Books), 151–152.

4. A. M. Starr to A. Bibo, October 13, 1970 (author's collection).

5. Interview with A. E. Roland, Wild Horse Mesa, New Mexico, July 2006.

CHAPTER 5. THE MILITARY PURSUIT

1. *Record of Engagements with Hostile Indians Within the Military Division of the Missouri, from 1868 to 1882* (Washington, DC: US Government Printing Office, 1882; repr. Bellevue, NE: The Old Army Press, 1969), extracted from pages 99 and 100, dealing with a part of the year 1882. Hereinafter referred to as "War Department summary, 1882."

2. Frances B. Heitman, *Historical Register and Dictionary of the United States Army, 1789–1903* (1903; reprint, Urbana: University of Illinois Press, 1965), 483.

3. War Department summary, 1882.

4. Dorothy Mazón to A. E. Roland, December 17, 2012.

5. War Department summary, 1882.

6. Marc Simmons, *The Little Lion of the Southwest* (Chicago: Swallow Press, 1973) 192–194.

7. Emphasis added. War Department summary, 1882.

8. Dan Thrapp, *Dateline Fort Bowie: Charles Fletcher Lummis Reports on an Apache War* (Norman: University of Oklahoma Press, 1979), 158.

9. Capt. Bean Commanding, Fort Craig, NM, August 2, 3 o'clock PM, to Acting Asst Adj. Gen. of the US Army, Santa Fe, NM. Letters Received by the Office of the Adjutant General Main Series 1881–1889, NARA.

10. Cleaveland, *No Life For A Lady*, 39.

11. Ball, *Indeh*, 62.

12. N. G. (Nicolás German) "Nick" Baca, interview by A. E. Roland, Quemado, NM, December 4, 2006.

13. *U. S. Buffalo Soldiers, Returns From Regular Army Cavalry Regiments, 1866–1916* (United States Ninth Cavalry, 1881–1887), Ancestry.com, 22 of 187; and *U. S. Registers of Deaths in the Regular Army, 1860–1889* (Register of Death of Regular Army, 1881 Jul–1882 Jun), Ancestry.com, 72 and 91 of 109.

14. War Department summary, 1882.

CHAPTER 6. THE AFTERMATH

1. Rosa Trujillo to Arty Bibo, personal communication, February 27, 1971 (author's collection).

2. *La Vega, Valencia County, New Mexico Territorial Census of 1885*, New Mexico Records Center and Archives, Santa Fe.

3. Schoolcraft et al., *Sacramental Records*, 199.

4. Charles H. Lange and Carroll L. Riley, eds. *The Southwestern Journals of Adolph F. Bandelier 1880–1882* (Albuquerque: University of New Mexico Press, 1966), 305, 317.

5. "The Story of Plácida Romero Pertaining to Her Experiences with the Indians," *Red River Chronicle* (Spanish edition), San Lorenzo, NM, May 13, 1882. Translated by Irma Belle Bibo Floersheim.

6. Col. Hatch at Ft. Cummings, NM, to Headquarters Department of Missouri at Ft. Garland, CO, August 16, 1881. Letters Received by the Office of the Adjutant General Main Series 1881–1889, NARA.

7. Col. Hatch to Gen. Pope and Adjt. Gen. of the US Army, August 16, 1881. Ibid.

8. Schoolcraft et al., *Sacramental Records*, 279.

9. This family information about Trinidad "Colorada" and Trinidad "La Apacha" was supplied by Anna Mae Starr (A. M. Starr to A. Bibo, October 13, 1970).

CHAPTER 7. VARIATIONS OF THE PLÁCIDA STORY

1. The author heard this three-year time period mentioned during one of Arty Bibo's interviews with Plácida's descendants.

2. Sherry Robinson, *Apache Voices* (Albuquerque: University of New Mexico Press, 2000), 9; and Paul Andrew Hutton, *The Apache Wars* (New York: Crown, 2016), 268.

3. Edwin R. Sweeney, *From Cochise to Geronimo: The Chiricahua Apaches, 1874–1886* (Norman: University of Oklahoma Press, 2010), 615n75, 659, and 660n37.

AFTERWORD: A LAGUNA CONNECTION by Leslie Marmon Silko

1. L. R. Bailey, *Indian Slave Trade in the Southwest* (Los Angeles: Westernlore Press, 1973), xv.

2. Ibid.

3. Ibid., 26.

4. Ibid., 19.

5. Ibid., 96.

6. Ibid., 93.

7. Ibid., 51.

8. Ibid., 122.

9. Ibid., 76–77.

10. Ibid., 128.

APPENDIX 8. LAS COSAS PERDIDAS DE RANCHO ARMIJO
by Carol A. Macaulay-Jameson

1. Bob Roland, personal communication, 2015.

2. US Bureau of the Census, 1880 Population Census. The ages of Antonio and Manuela at the time of their marriage in 1883: Antonio, 22, Valencia County, San Rafael, District 054; Manuela, 12, Valencia County, Cubero, District 054, https://www.ancestryheritagequest.com/imageviewer/collections/6742/images/4242011-00728?backlabel=ReturnSearchResults&queryId=b1657ab28669d9bd5d7f052810b6604f&pId=15459656.

3. US Bureau of the Census, 1900 Population Census. Antonio's age is listed as 37 and Manuela's age is listed as 30, Valencia County, Jaralozo, District 0175. Both Antonio and Manuela's ages conflict with the 1880 and the 1910 census records, https://www.ancestryheritagequest.com/imageviewer/collections/7602/images/4120507_00907?usePUB=true&_phsrc=dBp25&_phstart=successSource&usePUBJs=true&pId=48325162.

4. Richard Lee Nostrand, *The Hispano Homeland* (Norman: University of Oklahoma Press, 1996), 91.

5. Bob Roland, personal communication, 2015.

6. US Bureau of the Census, 1910 Population Census. Antonio's age is listed as 52 and his wife Manuelita as 48, Valencia County, San Rafael, District 0292, https://www.ancestryheritagequest.com/imageviewer/collections/7884/images/31111_4330942-01127?backlabel=ReturnSearchResults&queryId=294ea7cd9ed936babddee84e2cea7444&pId=16938239.

7. US Bureau of the Census, 1910 Population Census, Valencia County, Valencia, District 0289, https://www.ancestryheritagequest.com/imageviewer/collections/7884/images/31111_4330942-01041?backlabel=ReturnSearchResults&queryId=b3c168f71157ea70f118ccb215e072d0&pId=16937166.

8. Bob Roland, personal communication, 2015.

9. Bill Lindsey, "Bottle/Glass Colors," Society for Historical Archaeology, 2020, https://sha.org/bottle/colors.htm#Purple%20to%20Amethyst.

10. Bill Lindsey, "Bottle Bases," Society for Historical Archaeology, 2021, https://sha.org/bottle/bases.htm.

11. Bill Lindsey, "Bottle Finishes (aka 'Lips') and Closures," Society for Historical Archaeology, 2020, https://sha.org/bottle/finishes.htm.

12. Bill Lockhart, Beau Schreiver, Carol Serr, and Bill Lindsey, "Pitcher's and Fletcher's Castoria, An Uncommon Study of Common Bottles," in *Encyclopedia of Manufacturers Marks on Glass Containers*, Society for Historical Archaeology, 2019, https://sha.org/bottle/pdffiles/CastoriaHistory.pdf.

13. Bill Lindsey, "Bottle/Glass Colors," Society for Historical Archaeology, 2020, https://sha.org/bottle/colors.htm#Milk%20Glass.

14. Bill Lindsey, "Bottle Typing/Diagnostic Shapes, Food Bottles and Canning Jars," Society for Historical Archaeology, 2021, https://sha.org/bottle/food.htm.

15. Ibid.

16. Georgeanna H. Greer, *American Stonewares: The Art and Craft of Utilitarian Potters* (Exton, PA: Schiffer Publishing Limited, 1981).

17. AntiqueMarks.com, "What Are Antique Marks?," 2021, https://antique-marks.com/antique-marks.html.

18. Jonathan Weiland, "A Comparison and Review of Window Glass Analysis Approaches in Historical Archaeology," *Technical Briefs in Historical Archaeology* 4, no. 2 (2009): 31.

19. PicClick.com, "Antique Brass Work Clothes Overall Button 'Jumbo Make' w/ Elephant - 11/16 in.," 2021, https://picclick.com/Antique-Brass-Work-Clothes-Overall-Button-Jumbo-Make-382468936625.html; Antolijs Venovcevs, *Dress for Life and Death: The Archaeology of Common Nineteenth-Century Buttons* (Toronto: Archaeological Services Inc., 2013).

20. David D. Kowalski, ed., *Standard Catalog of Winchester: The Most Comprehensive Price Guide Ever Published* (Iola, WI: Krause Publications, 2000).

21. Denise Van Patten, "Introduction to Bisque and Porcelain Dolls," 2019, https://www.thesprucecrafts.com/bisque-and-porcelain-dolls-774692; Catherine Christopher, *The Complete Book of Doll Making and Collecting* (Mineola: Dover Publications, 1971), 187–190.

22. Wikipedia, "Gallup, New Mexico," 2021, https://en.wikipedia.org/wiki/Gallup,_New_Mexico.

23. David F. Myrick, *New Mexico's Railroads: A Historical Survey* (Albuquerque: University of New Mexico Press, 1990).

24. Nostrand, 110–112.

25. Bob Roland, personal communication, 2015; US Bureau of the Census, 1910 Population Census, Valencia County, Cubero, District 0287, https://www.ancestryheritagequest.com/imageviewer/collections/7884/images/31111_4330942-00979?usePUB=true&_phsrc=dBp28&_phstart=successSource&usePUBJs=true&pId=16936521.

BIBLIOGRAPHY

ARCHIVAL DOCUMENTS

Cubero, Valencia County, New Mexico Territory, *U. S. Census of 1870*. New Mexico Records Center and Archives, Santa Fe.

Cubero, Valencia County, New Mexico Territory, *U. S. Census of 1880*. New Mexico Records Center and Archives, Santa Fe.

La Vega, Valencia County. *New Mexico Territorial Census of 1885*. New Mexico Records Center and Archives, Santa Fe.

Letters Received by the Office of the Adjutant General Main Series 1881–1889 (US Army). File 4746, Adjutant General's Office 1881, Roll 44, Microcopy 689, Records of the Adjutant General's Office, Record Group 94. Washington, DC: National Archives and Records Administration, 1985. Microfilm in author's collection.

U. S. Buffalo Soldiers, Returns From Regular Army Cavalry Regiments, 1866–1916, United States Ninth Cavalry, 1881–1887. Ancestry.com, 22 of 187.

U. S. Registers of Deaths in the Regular Army, 1860–1889. Registers of Deaths of Regular Army, 1881 Jul–1882 Jun. Ancestry.com, 72 and 91 of 109.

BOOKS

Adams, David Wallace. *Three Roads to Magdalena*. Lawrence: University Press of Kansas, 2016.

Bailey, L. R. *Indian Slave Trade in the Southwest*. Los Angeles, CA: Westernlore Press, 1973.

Ball, Eve. *In the Days of Victorio: Recollections of a Warm Springs Apache*. Tucson, University of Arizona Press, 1970.

———. *Indeh, An Apache Odyssey*. Provo, UT: Brigham Young University Press, 1980.

Cleaveland, Agnes Morley. *No Life for a Lady*. Boston: Houghton Mifflin Co., 1941.

Cleaveland, Norman. *The Morleys*. Albuquerque, NM: Calvin Horn Publisher, 1971.

Espinosa, Gilberto, and Tibo J. Chávez. *El Río Abajo*. Pampa, TX: Pampa Print Shop, 1965.

Fierman, Floyd S. *Guts and Ruts: The Jewish Pioneer on the Trail in the American Southwest*. New York: KTAV Publishing House, 1985.

Goodwin, Grenville, and Neil Goodwin. *The Apache Diaries.* Lincoln: University of Nebraska Press, 2000.

Gunn, John M. *Schat-Chen: History Traditions and Narratives of the Queres Indians of Laguna and Acoma*. Albuquerque, NM: Albright & Anderson, 1917.

Heitman, Francis B. *Historical Register and Dictionary of the United States Army, 1789–1903.* Washington, DC: Government Printing Office, 1903; reprint, Urbana: University of Illinois Press, 1965.

Hutton, Paul Andrew. *The Apache Wars*. New York: Crown, 2016.

Johnston, Langford R. *Old Magdalena Cow Town.* Albuquerque, NM: Cottonwood Printing Co., 1983.

Julyan, Robert. *The Place Names of New Mexico.* Albuquerque: University of New Mexico Press, 1998.

Kemp, Ben W. *Cow Dust and Saddle Leather*. Norman: University of Oklahoma Press, 1968.

Lamadrid, Enrique R. "La Pasión de Plácida Romero: The Poetics of Faith, Authority, and Remembrance of a Cautiva and her Ballad." Unpublished manuscript, December 2010. Hard copy in author's collection.

Lange, Charles H., and Carroll. L. Riley, eds. *The Southwestern Journals of Adolph F. Bandelier 1880–1882*. Albuquerque: University of New Mexico Press, 1966.

Lee, Susan E. *These Also Served*. Los Lunas, NM: Book Craftsmen Associates, 1960.

Lekson, Stephen H. *Nana's Raid: Apache Warfare in Southern New Mexico, 1881*. El Paso: Texas Western Press, 1987.

Lummis, Charles F. *General Crook and the Apache Wars.* Flagstaff, AZ: Northland Press, 1966.

McGaw, William Cochran. *Savage Scene: The Life and Times of James Kirker, Frontier King.* New York: Hastings House, 1972; reprint, San Lorenzo, NM: High-Lonesome Books, 1989.

Park, John R. *New Mexico Mining Heritage Guide.* Version 1.2.3. South Miami, FL: Stonerose Publishing Co., 2003.

Parish, William J. *The Charles Ilfeld Company: A Study of the Rise and Decline of Mercantile Capitalism in New Mexico*. Cambridge, MA: Harvard University Press, 1961.

Pearce, T. M., ed. *New Mexico Place Names: A Geographical Dictionary.* Albuquerque: University of New Mexico Press, 1965.

Rathbun, Daniel C. B. and David B. Alexander. *New Mexico Frontier Military Place Names.* Las Cruces, NM: Yucca Tree Press, 2003.

Robinson, Sherry. *Apache Voices.* Albuquerque: University of New Mexico Press, 2000.

Schoolcraft, Edward J., et al. *Sacramental Records from the Archives of the Diocese of Gallup: New Mexico Marriages; San Jose de la Laguna, 1777–1892; Nuestra Señora de los Delores, 1852–1889; San Rafael, Seboyeta, Gallup, 1890–1904; Gallup Cathedral, 1904–1922.* Albuquerque, NM: Hispanic Genealogical Research Center, 2002.

Silko, Leslie Marmon. *Storyteller.* New York: Seaver Books, 1981.

Simmons, Marc. *The Little Lion of the Southwest.* Chicago: Swallow Press, 1973.

Stratton, Porter A. *The Territorial Press of New Mexico, 1834–1912.* Albuquerque: University of New Mexico Press, 1969.

Sweeney, Edwin R. *From Cochise to Geronimo: The Chiricahua Apaches, 1874–1886.* Norman: University of Oklahoma Press, 2010.

Thompson, Jerry D. *Desert Tiger: Captain Paddy Graydon and the Civil War in the Far Southwest*, Southwestern Studies Series, no. 97. El Paso: Texas Western Press, 1992.

Thrapp, Dan L. *The Conquest of Apacheria.* Norman: University of Oklahoma Press, 1967.

———. *Dateline Fort Bowie: Charles Fletcher Lummis Reports on an Apache War.* Norman: University of Oklahoma Press, 1979.

Tietjen, Gary L. *Encounter with the Frontier.* Los Alamos, NM: self-published, 1969.

US War Department. *Record of Engagements with Hostile Indians Within the Military Division of the Missouri, from 1868 to 1882.* Compiled from official records. Washington, DC: Government Printing Office, 1882.

ARTICLES

Miller, Harold. "Nana's Raid of 1881." *Password* 19, no. 2 (Summer 1974): 51–70.

Shuman, Amy. "Entitlement and Empathy in Personal Narrative." *Narrative Inquiry* 16, no. 1 (2006): 149.

Starr, Anna Mae. "Plácida Romero: La Cautiva." *La Herencia del Norte* (Summer 1999): 14–15.

Vaden, Clay W. *Mexican Boy Captured by Apache Indians.* Pioneer story from the WPA Writer's Project, 1936–1940. http://htg-is.vianet/~artpike/quemado.htlm.

INTERVIEWS/LETTERS: IN AUTHOR'S COLLECTION

Rosa Trujillo interviews by Arthur Bibo: Summer 1966, Albuquerque, NM; October 17, 1969, Albuquerque, NM; December 3, 1969, Cubero, NM.

Corrido authentication note from Rosa Trujillo to Arthur Bibo, October 1, 1969, Albuquerque, NM.

Anna Mae Starr letter to Arthur Bibo, October 13, 1970.

Margaret Johnson (Aragón), grandniece of and writing for Rosa Trujillo, letter to Arthur Bibo, February 27, 1971.

Norman Cleaveland interview by A. E. Roland, September 29, 1979, Cleaveland Ranch at Dátil Canyon, NM.

Buddy Major interview by A. E. Roland, July 14, 2006, Wild Horse Mesa, NM.

N. G. Baca interview by A. E. Roland, December 4, 2006, Quemado, NM.

Dorothy Mazón letter to A. E. Roland, December 17, 2012.

INDEX

Page numbers in *italics* refer to illustrations.

Abeyta y Romero, Rafael, 17
Acoma Pueblo/people, 9, 25–27, 31, 34, 43, 52–54, 63, 65, 81, 97, 125n1
Acts of the Legislative Assembly of the Territory of New Mexico (1882), 61, 69, 104–5
Alamo Canyon, 55
Alamo Navajos, 44, 59, 71–72
Alamocita Creek, 31, 44–45, 57–58, 72, 111, 126n10
Alamosa, 39, 44–45, 110–11
Albuquerque Daily Journal, 29, 31, 58, 65, 110–12
Albuquerque, New Mexico, 9, 26, 31, 64, 68–69, 73, 108, 116
Alcón Canyon, 43–44
A'mooh (Laguna woman), 75–76
antipeonage law, 8–9
La Apacha. *See* Romero, María Trinidad "La Apacha"
Apaches: abduct Plácida, 12–14, 25, 34–35, 40–41, 63, 73–75, 102, 104, 106, 122n10; attack Rancho Cebolla, 7, 37, 39–41; and Indian slave trade, 8, 11–12, 73–75; kill/kidnap Rancho García settlers, 31; Mexico stronghold of, 47, *48*, 51, 74–75, 79; military pursuit of, 55–60, 64–65, 70, 85, 110–12; murder Domingo, 25, 31, 35, 40–41, 52–53, 63, 74, 104; newspaper reports on, 110–12; Plácida escapes from, 49, 51–52, 75, 101–6; pursued by Laguna Regulars, 75–76; pursued by Mexicans, 7, 122n11; recruit Navajos, 71–72; routes of, 31, 32–33, 81; San Joaquín rancheria of, 47, 49, 50, 70–71; scalps of, 49, 75; take Plácida to Mexico, 43–47, 69–70; women help Plácida escape, 51–52, 75, 79, 122n11. *See also* Nana's Raid; Warm Springs Apaches
archaeological survey, 84, 113–17
Armijo, Antonio, 26, 65, 99, 113–17, 129n2–3, 129n6
Armijo, Manuelita. *See* Gallegos, Manuela "Manuelita"

Baca, Ignacio, 57, 126n10
Baca, Juan de Dios, 20, 32, 45–46, 112

Baca, N. G., 58
Baca, New Mexico, 67, 79
Baca, Timoteo, 32, 57–58, 104
Baca, Ygnacio, 20, 32, 45–46, 112, 126n10
Ballad of Plácida Romero, The. *See* Corrido de Plácida Romero
ballads, 7. *See also* El Corrido de Timoteo Baca; Corrido de Plácida Romero; *inditas*
Bandelier, Adolph, 34, 62
Barnes, Sidney A., 63, 106
Barth, Solomon, 59
Bennett, Frank, 56
Bernalillo, New Mexico, 25, 73, 97
Bibo, Arthur "Arty," 13, *24*, 27, 41, 117; and Acoma Pueblo, 26, 34; biography of, 25–27, 97–98; death of, 9, 28–29, 68; hears Plácida's story in childhood, 26, 69; original ballad given to, 28, 34, 65, 84, 87, 123n3; ranch of, 9, 25–27, 34–35, 65, 81, 97; researches Plácida's ballad, 9, 15, 26–29, 34–35, 52–53, 66–67, 82, 84, 113
Bibo, Emil, 25–26, 65, 97, 117
Bibo, Irma, 26, 29, 117
Bibo, Nathan, 26
Bibo, Phillip, 26, 54, 117
Bibo Ranch, 54, 64, 81
Bibo, Simon, 34
Bibo, Solomon, 26
Bledsoe, Mary Daley, 84
Blue Water Vega, 7, 32–33, 41, 52, 63, 82, 122n5
Brito, Pablo, 35, 52
Brito, Petronilo Martínez y, 52
Buenaventura, Mexico, 22, 47, 51, 70–71, 102, 122n11
Buffalo Soldiers, 29, 40, 43–45
Bureau of Indian Affairs, 62
Bureau of Land Management, 54, 59

Campo Santo Viejo de Cubero, 65–66, 67
Cañón del Cristo, 51, 101–2, 122n11
captivity narratives, 12–16
Carrizo Canyon, 32, 44–45, 59, 111
Catholic Church, 8, 66, 73, 75–76, 79, 122n7
Cebolla Canyon, 29, 35, 37, *38*, 39–40, 43, 52, 58, 60, 64, 74
Cebolla Ranch. *See* Rancho Cebolla
Cebolla Springs, 40, 44, 54, 110

Cebolla Springs Ranch. *See* Rancho Cebolla
Cebolleta, 43, 52, 61, 73
Cebollita Canyon, 35, 113
Cebollita Mesa, 40, 53
Cebollita Valley, *24*, 34, 52, 54, 65
Cerro Escoba, 20, 37, 41, 43, 52
Chávez, José, 68, 99
Chávez, José Angel, 59
Chávez, Manuel Antonio, 56
Chávez, Trinidad Romero. *See* Romero, María Trinidad "La Apacha"
Chihuahua, México, 7, 39, 47, *48*, 49, 51, 60, 63, 74–75, 79, 101, 103, 105
Chiricahuas, 44, 70–71, 125n6
church records, 61, 66, 69, 73, 76, 122n8
Ciénega Ranch, 44–45, 59, 111
Civil War, 8, 56
Cleaveland, Agnes Morley, 57
Corrido de Plácida Romero, 9; and Baca murder scene, 45–46; and capture of Plácida, 37, 64; English translation of, 17–23, 28–29, 81; given to Arty Bibo, 28, 34, 65, 84, 87, 123n3; Mexican place names in, 47, *48*, 49; music for, 17, 25, 84, 121n2; original transcription of, 15–23, 27, 28, 34–35, 54, 65, 69, 84, 87–96, 122n9, 123n3; passed on verbally, 7, 12, 15, 54; performances of, 15–16, 26, 28, 31, 34, 65, 84, 113; and Plácida's escape, 51–52; researching of, 26–29, 31, 34–35, 37, 39–41, 43–47, 51–53, 57–59, 69–72; Spanish version of, 15–23, 25, 28, 34, 54, 122n9; unsequenced version of, 15; variations of, 69–72, 84, 121n2; writing of, 12–14
El Corrido de Timoteo Baca, 58
Crónica del Río Colorado. See Red River Chronicle
Cubero Land Grant, 13
Cubero, New Mexico, 31, 112; Armijo family in, 113; Arty Bibo's life in, 13, 25–26, 35, 69, 97; Bandelier's stay in, 62; Catholic Church in, 122n7; Fiesta de San Lorenzo in, 37, 39–40, 70; mercantile in, 115, 117; patron saint of, 37, 121n4; Plácida gives affidavit in, 13, 69; Plácida returns to, 7, 53–54, 61–62, 69–70, 75, 79; and Plácida's ballad, 7, 17–20, 25–26, 34–35, 65, 69; Plácida's burial in, 9, 65–66, 67; rescue party of, 51–52, 70–71, 123n12; search party of, 58; as slave-trading center, 8, 73–74

Daly, George, 60
Dátil Mountains, 56–57, 81, 110–11

Eastman, Galen, 13–14, 62–64, 75, 106–9
El Paso, Texas, 51, 69, 73, 80, 101

Floersheim, Irma Belle Bibo, 29. *See also* Bibo, Irma
Florida Mountains, *48*
Fort Defiance, 62, 75, 108
freighters, 31, 32–33, 57–58, 72
French Camp, 111

Galeana, Mexico, 47, *48*, 49, 71
Gallegos, Domingo: family of, 39, 99–100, 113, 122n8, 124n2; gravesite of, 52–53, 58; marriage of, 99–100, 124n1; murder of, 7, 25, 37, 39–41, 61–63, 65, 74, 104, 106, 121n4; Plácida seeks justice for, 12–13; and Plácida's ballad, 17–19, 40, 65; pocket-knife of, 65, 84; Procopio García and, 61, 70; and Rancho Cebolla, 39, 124n4
Gallegos, Felipa, 37, 99–100, 122n8, 124n2
Gallegos, Manuela "Manuelita," 129n2–3, 129n6; attends Fiesta de San Lorenzo, 37, 70, 122n8; daughter of, 65, 84; family of, 99, 113, 124n2; homestead of, 26, 65, 113–17; marriage of, 113, 122n8; and Plácida's ballad, 21
Gallegos, María Plácida Romero. *See* Romero, Plácida
Gallegos, Trinidad "Colorada": abduction of, 29, 31, 35, 40, 58, 61–63, 65, 70, 74, 106–7; birth/death of, 68, 99, 124n2; and half-sister Trinidad "La Apacha," 61, 67–68, 70, 75, 79–80; left with Navajos, 41, 52, 60, 63–64, 70, 75, 79; life with Navajos, 9, 64, 67–68, 75; Plácida tries to recover, 13–14, 66, 106; and Plácida's ballad, 17, 20–22, 65
García, Procopio, 14, 22, 43, 51–52, 61, 69–70, 102, 104–5
García, Ramón, 57–58
genealogy records, 13, 37, 56, 66–67, 69, 84
Geronimo, 25, 39, 75–76
Gonzales, María Acacia, 19, 22, 122n5
Grants, New Mexico, 9, 25, 27, 31, 34, 64, 69, 115
Güero (Navajo man), 14, 63
Guilfoyle, John Francis, 40, 55–56, 58, 110
Gunn, John, 44
Gutiérrez, María, 17, 54

Indian Claims Act of 1946, 97
Indian scouts, 46, 55–56, 59–60, 64, 70–71
Indian Wars, 12, 25
inditas, 15–17

Jaralosa Canyon, 113
Juana (Navajo captive), 76–80

Kessell, John L., 27, 97
Kirker, James, 49

Ków-ina Spring, 34–35
Laguna Pueblo/people, 25, 64–65, 75–80, 82–83, 110, 112, 125n2
Laguna Regulars, 75–76
Lamadrid, Enrique R., 15–16, 81, 83–84
Las Cruces, New Mexico, 29, 51, 61, 103, 108
Las Vegas, New Mexico, 14, 63, 106
Lillie (Laguna woman), 76–78
Little Cebolla Spring, 36, 37
Los Lunas, New Mexico, 77–78
Los Pilares Ranch, 9, 26–27, 34, 54, 81, 97, 113, 117
Los Pilares Valley, 27, 34, 54, 65, 113–17
Lozen (Apache woman), 71
Luera Springs, 110–12

Macauly-Jameson, Carol, 84, 113–17
Major, Buddy, 53–54, 81
El Malpais, 9, 34, 54
Mangas Coloradas (Apache chief), 39, 70
Mangus (Apache war chief), 39, 69–71
Manuelito (Navajo chief), 8
Margarito (Navajo man), 63, 106
Marmon, Leland "Lee," 36, 38, 42, 82, 110
Marmon, Robert G., and Walter G., 64, 75–76, 110, 112
Marmon Silko, Leslie, 11, 73–80, 82–83
McCartys, 31, 34, 64, 110, 112
McWhorter, Mike, 81, 111
Mesa del Oro, 42, 43–44, 52
Mescaleros, 55, 71
Mexican Consulate, 51, 101
Mexicans, 110; captivity stories and, 12–13; and Indian slave trade, 11, 74, 77–78; killed by Apaches, 55–56; pursue Apaches, 7, 112, 122n11; slaughter Apaches, 7, 39, 71; and war with Indians, 8, 11
Mexico: Apache stronghold in, 74–75, 79; Apaches escape to, 39, 60; independence from Spain, 74; Plácida escapes from, 14, 25, 49, 51–52, 61, 63, 69–71, 101–6; Plácida taken to, 25, 43–47, 61, 63, 69–70, 106
military reports, 55–56, 58–60, 62, 69–71
Mónica Springs, 32, 55–56, 71, 110
Museum of New Mexico (Santa Fe), 87

Nana (Apache chief), 62, 84–85, 123n4, 125n6; as Apache chief, 7, 30, 39; attacks Rancho Cebolla, 34, 72; avenges death of Victorio, 7, 25, 31, 39; captures Plácida, 12, 104; divides his forces, 31, 43, 65, 72; escapes to Mexico, 43–44, 47, 48, 51, 70; evades military pursuit, 41, 56; kills ranchers/freighters, 31, 57; and Plácida's ballad, 18, 69–71, 121n3; raiding party of, 69–72, 122n11; raids Rancho García, 31, 43, 51, 72

Nana's Raid, 7, 9, 25, 29, 31, 32–33, 34, 44, 49, 55–61, 125n2, 126n10
National Archives and Records Administration (Washington, DC), 26
Navajos, 56–59; attack/raid on Rancho Cebolla, 7, 37, 39–41, 72; and Indian slaves/slave trade, 8, 73–74, 76–79; and the Long Walk, 8, 44; military pursuit of, 78, 110–11; mistreated by Indian agent, 62–64, 75, 106–9; and Plácida's affidavit, 14, 41, 63, 106; Plácida's daughter left with, 41, 52, 62, 79, 123n12; Plácida's daughter raised by, 9, 64, 67–68, 75, 79; recruited by Nana, 71–72
New Mexico Historical Review, 27, 85, 98
New Mexico Records Center and Archives (Santa Fe), 26
New Mexico Territory: Americans migrate to, 116–17; courts of, 12, 74; and Indian slave trade, 11–12, 74, 79–80; legislature of, 8, 12, 14, 61, 69; merchants of, 82, 116–17
newspaper accounts, 14, 29, 34, 44, 49, 51–52, 58, 61–66, 69, 71, 75, 101–12
No Life for a Lady (Cleaveland), 57
nuevomexicanos, 8, 12, 14

Ojo Apache, 32, 42, 43
Ojo (Ojito) Salado, 20, 32, 42, 43
Otero, Gregorio N., 13–14, 62–63, 66–67, 69, 106, 121n4
Otero, Melquiades, 17, 54, 67

Palomas, Mexico, 47
Parker, Charles, 39, 44–45, 58–59, 110–11
los partidos, 39
El Progresista, 29, 49, 51, 71, 84, 102–3
Pueblo Revolt of 1680, 37, 73

railroads, 31, 34, 64, 116–17
Rancho Cebolla, 29, 44, 84; Apaches attack on, 7, 31, 34, 37, 39–41, 69–70, 72; burials at, 52–53; location of, 32–33; murders at, 25, 31, 40–41, 51, 57–58, 63, 70, 122n8; owner of, 39, 124n4; Plácida kidnapped at, 40–41, 102; and Plácida's ballad, 18, 53; ruins of, 36, 38, 53–54
Rancho García, 31, 32, 43, 51, 57, 59, 61, 64, 70, 72, 125n2
Red Canyon, 56–57, 111
Red River Chronicle, 14, 63–64, 106–8, 121n4
Río Grande Republican, 29, 51, 103, 108–9
Río Grande River, 7–8, 44–45, 55, 71, 73, 126n5
Río Salado, 44–45, 52, 59, 111
Roland, Aulton E. "Bob," 9, 13, 113, 116–17
Romero, Calletano, 13, 21, 37, 52, 58, 64, 66–67, 69–70, 84, 121n2, 122n9

Romero, Manuela Gallegos. *See* Gallegos, Manuela "Manuelita"
Romero, María Trinidad "La Apacha," 61, 67–68, 75, 79–80, 99, 123n12
Romero, Pedro Molina, 19, 21–22, 122n9
Romero, Plácida, 9, 59; abduction of, 7, 58, 65, 70–71, 73–75, 85, 102; affidavit of, 14, 41, 53, 62–63, 66, 69–71, 121n4, 125n5; on Baca murders, 20, 45–46; captivity of, 12–14, 25–29, 31, 34–35, 37, 39–41, 122n9–10; children of, 37, 65, 70, 99–100, 113, 122n8–9, 124n2; death/burial of, 65–66, 67; descendants of, 26, 31, 34, 55–56, 66, 68–69, 84, 87, 99–100; escape of, 49, 51–54, 61, 63, 69–71, 101–6, 122n10; family of, 56, 61, 99–100; freed by Apache women, 51–52, 75, 79, 122n11; on husband's murder, 18–19, 40; jewelry box of, 65, 66, 84; marriages of, 61, 66, 79, 99–100, 124n1; on the Navajos, 106–7; parents of, 19, 21–22, 122n5, 122n9; performs her ballad, 16, 65; photograph of, 27; rape of, 61, 68, 75, 79; returns from captivity, 53–54, 61–62, 66, 69–70, 75, 123n12; search party sent for, 58; story of, 12–13, 25–26, 54, 69–72, 79; taken to Mexico, 43–47, 61, 63, 69, 106; and transcribing of ballad, 15; treated badly by Apaches, 49, 52; tries to recover daughter, 62–64, 75, 79, 106, 123n12; visited by Bandelier, 62; visits husband's grave, 52–53
Romero, Policarpio, 66, 67
Romero, Victor, 52, 61, 66, 100

San Fidel, New Mexico, 54, 61, 65, 69
San Joaquín Cañón, 23, 47, 48, 49, 50, 71
San Joaquín rancheria, 47, 49, 50, 70–71
San Lorenzo, 17–19, 37, 39, 70, 121n4
San Mateo Mountains, 55–56, 62, 75, 111, 126n5
San Rafael, New Mexico, 39, 43, 69, 102, 113
Santa Fe New Mexican, 29, 51, 101–2

Santa Fe, New Mexico, 8, 61–62, 73, 81, 87, 105
Seboyeta, New Mexico, 8, 25, 29, 43, 69, 124n1
sheep ranchers, 31, 33, 57, 72
Sheldon, Lionel, 14, 51, 62, 66, 101
slavery/slave trade, 7–9, 11–14, 21, 44, 51, 73–80
Smith, G. W., 60
Smouse, Don and Fern, 68
Socorro, New Mexico, 45, 83, 112, 126n10
Spanish, the, 7–8, 73–74, 78–79
Starr, Anna Mae, 39, 52, 84, 122n9, 124n5

Taos, New Mexico, 8, 73, 80
Treaty of Guadalupe Hidalgo, 11
Tres Castillos, 7, 39, 51, 71
Trujillo, Felipe, 15, 28, 99, 123n2
Trujillo, Rosa, 13, 27, 28, 61, 65–66, 71, 84, 87, 121n2, 123n2–3

University of New Mexico Zimmerman Library, 26, 106
US government, 8–9, 62–64, 74
US military, 8, 11–12, 39–41, 43–47, 52, 55, 58–60, 64–65, 70, 77, 108–11. *See also* Buffalo Soldiers
US War Department, 55–56, 58–60, 62

Valencia County, New Mexico, 31, 44, 61–64, 104, 106–7
Vargas, José María, 7, 19, 37, 39–41, 52–53, 104, 106, 124n5
Victorio (Apache chief), 7, 25, 31, 39, 51, 55, 57, 71, 84–85, 102

Warm Springs Apaches, 30, 39–41, 71, 125n6
Watt, Robert N. "Bob," 84–85
Whittington, Josephine Romero, 77–78
Wright, Harry, 110

Ysleta, Texas, 51, 70–71